Divine Feminine Handbook

Volume II

Unleash Your Inner Goddess

MARILYN PABON

BALBOA.PRESS

A DIVISION OF HAY HOUSE

Balboa Press books may be ordered through booksellers or by contacting:

Balboa Press
A Division of Hay House
1663 Liberty Drive
Bloomington, IN 47403
www.balboapress.com
844-682-1282

Because of the dynamic nature of the Internet, any web addresses or links contained in this book may have changed since publication and may no longer be valid. The views expressed in this work are solely those of the author and do not necessarily reflect the views of the publisher, and the publisher hereby disclaims any responsibility for them.

The author of this book does not dispense medical advice or prescribe the use of any technique as a form of treatment for physical, emotional, or medical problems without the advice of a physician, either directly or indirectly. The intent of the author is only to offer information of a general nature to help you in your quest for emotional and spiritual well-being. In the event you use any of the information in this book for yourself, which is your constitutional right, the author and the publisher assume no responsibility for your actions.

Any people depicted in stock imagery provided by Getty Images are models, and such images are being used for illustrative purposes only. Certain stock imagery © Getty Images.

Print information available on the last page.

ISBN: 978-1-9822-6809-1 (sc)
ISBN: 978-1-9822-6810-7 (e)

Balboa Press rev. date: 04/30/2021

INTRODUCTION

Unleashing Your Inner Goddess is about understanding and acknowledging that her divinity exists. Your Inner Goddess is the purest form of you. She is everything love and never concerns herself with trivial things. She's been around for a LONG time, and knows the ways of the Universe. She also knows why you're here! She is your Divine spark.

We often make the mistake of thinking our history begins with our birth in this life and that our memories extend only from the moment of our birth. Our physical body is just the tip of the iceberg when it comes to who we are and what makes us, us. We have memories and knowledge from our life/lives before this one. Your Inner Goddess is your soul, your true essence, who always wants the best for you. She's the part of you who truly remembers who you were before you came to this world. She's free and wild and really doesn't care about other people's opinions. She's the part of you who's at peace with what you've been through and where you're headed.

It's "You" who set the course of your life and the things you want to accomplish and learn, before you even came to this earth. It's "You" whispering guidance to yourself about your highest path and purpose. Your Inner Goddess invariably involves how you can best serve others while being true to yourself. This part of You helps you to keep on track with your life's purpose and in touch with your passions and joy. Your Inner Goddess has brought with her your feminine energy. She's that part of your soul who is fully connected with the Divine Feminine. Your Inner Goddess manifests as your higher self, your soul, your spirit, your intuition, the eternal essence of who you truly are.

You might frequently hear the phrase "finding yourself", but finding yourself is really returning to yourself and to her. Tapping into this divine feminine energy allows you to live life guided by your true self and be in perfect flow with the magic of the universe.

Every woman has an Inner Goddess, whether you realize it or not. Connecting with your Inner Goddess will automatically make you feel happier, radiant, healthier, and sexier! Your higher vibration will make you naturally glow from the inside out.

You don't need to contact your Higher Self as an entity outside of yourself, she is You! Wisdom and memories are inside of you, if you will access them. Pay attention to your desires and passions. Your truest, heartfelt desires are feedback from your Inner Goddess about what you want to do now. Living from your Inner Goddess means not sacrificing or ignoring those desires, it also means listening to those desires on a daily basis.

You know you are stepping into your Goddess self and awakening your true eternal nature when you become more concerned about you inner journey than your outward one.

"Divine Feminine Handbook" is a four-book series:
Volume I: Overcoming Self-Doubt
Volume II: Unleashing Your Inner Goddess
Volume III: Extreme Feminine Self-Care
Volume IV: Self-Reliance in a Changing World

CONTENTS

CHAPTER 1

The Spiritual Goddess

"The Goddess doesn't enter us from outside; she emerges from deep within. She is not held back by what happened in the past. She is conceived in consciousness, born in love, and nurtured by higher thinking. She is integrity and value, created and sustained by the hard work of personal growth and the discipline of a life lived actively in hope." Marianne Williamson

In spirit your Inner Goddess is your soul, your spirit, your true essence, your intuition. She's been around for a LONG time, and knows the ways of the Universe. She's your Divine spark!

In human form a goddess is the divine creator of life, she is intentional, creative, and free. She doesn't judge herself or others. She sees life as a spiritual engagement, an interconnected web of diverse energies emitted by people, animals, stones, plants, and trees. She engages with others on spiritual terms, and honors every life force as sacred. No two goddesses look alike, think alike or act alike because each is the manifestation of a unique soul.

What More is a Goddess?

- A woman who is in the process of learning to accept and love herself on all levels, body, mind and spirit.
- A woman who because she focuses on personal growth and self-awareness, experiences a life increasingly filled with peace, love, joy, passion, and fun.
- A woman who understands she has unlimited capacity to make her life anything she wants.
- A woman who is inspired to give to those around her because of her sense of gratitude and abundance.
- A woman who infuses life with magic and ritual.
- A woman who inspires others to access their divine power.

Benefits of Awakening and Unleashing Your Inner Goddess

- Connecting to your higher self
- Increased love for yourself and others
- Heightened intuition
- Experience more joy and purpose
- Ability to Let Go
- More self-compassion and confidence

Goddess Practices

- She works on lunar cycles because those mirror her own body's rhythm.
- She keeps stones chosen for specific purposes in her pockets and pillowcases.
- She uses essential oils, incense, herbs and gem-infused candles to raise associated energies.
- She drinks tea as medicine and views bath as ritual.

- She chooses her jewelry and adornment with care, and dresses in a manner that flatters her body and reflects her wild spirit.
- She Creates Sacred Space: Treat your space as your temple. Declutter and remove items that you don't love, or you aren't using. Smudge often. Create intention and bring beauty to your space.
- She Connects to the Divine Within: Take time for you. Meditate, breathe, exercise, garden, cook, create art, or do anything which connects yourself, to your own Divinity. I garden and grow flowers, herbs, fruits and veggies to connect with the Divine; time in my gardens is sweet medicine.
- She Lets Go and Let Goddess: Choose your battles wisely. Whatever we hold onto, we give energy to. Let go of what does not serve you. Let go of what you cannot control. Remember you are wise but not omnipotent and you not need to solve other people's problems, that is not why you are here.
- She Reconnects With Mother Nature and Grandmother Moon: Spend time in Nature, bask under the moon, partake in ritual, grow your herbs and plants, hike, swim, and play outdoors. Do what feeds your soul.
- She Embraces and Asserts Her Divine Feminine Power: Don't be afraid to take charge when life requires it. Empower yourself, and speak your truth with love and compassion to those who need to hear your voice. Remember that sometimes the person who needs your truth most is you.

If the process of becoming more goddess-like seems overwhelming to you, take one small step at a time. We will dive deeper into each of the above throughout the book. Get a special journal dedicated for your Goddess journey. Take the things you resinate with and leave the rest behind. Enjoy the journey.

Spirituality

Those who develop and maintain a spiritual practice that aligns with their cultural and spiritual beliefs will enjoy longer, healthier and happier lives.

Spirituality is the freedom and ability to find your own personal path to your purpose and meaning on earth and the here-after. It is about your ability to experience direct personal revelation.

We are each unique and individual, we have had different life experiences and formed our own perspectives. The Divine Feminine will attract similar souls and united will be a strong force of change for the betterment of humans, animals, the plant world and Mother Earth.

Your Inner Goddess invariably involves how you can best serve others while being true to yourself. You will be surprised how much universal support you garner when you bring a greater spiritual meaning to your physical experience.

Connecting To Your Inner Goddess

"You must learn to get in touch with your inner most being. This true essence is beyond the ego. It is fearless; it is free; it is immune to criticism; it does not fear any challenge. It is beneath no one, superior to no one, and full of magic, mystery and enchantment." Deepak Chora

We often make the mistake of thinking our history begins with our birth in this life and that our memories extend only from the moment of our birth. Our physical body is just the tip of the iceberg when it comes to who we are and what makes us, us. We all have a soul, which is sometimes called your spirit, your Higher Self, and your Inner Goddess.

It's "You" who set the course of your life and the things you came to earth to learn, before you even arrived here on earth.

It's "You" whispering guidance to yourself about your highest path and purpose. This part of you helps you to keep on track with your life purpose and in touch with your passions and joy.

Women use to be the Keepers of Knowledge in almost all societies around the world; that ancient legacy resides in your DNA. It speaks to you in quiet whispers known as "women's intuition".

You don't need to contact your Higher Self as an entity outside of you, it is You! You have wisdom and memories inside of you, if you will access them.

Pay attention to your desires, interests and passions. Your truest, heartfelt desires are feedback from your Inner Goddess about what you want to do now. Living from your Inner Goddess means not sacrificing or ignoring those desires. It also means listening to those desires on a daily basis.

Your soul, your inner goddess, is the purest form of you. She is everything love and never concerns herself with trivial things. She's your Divine spark!

Meditate To Quiet Your Mind

"I have been a seeker and still am, but I stopped asking the books and the stars. I started listening to the teaching of my soul." Rumi

The quickest way to practice accessing your soul, your Inner Goddess, is meditation. It quiets the mind and the chatter and takes you straight to the quiet and calm of your inner self.

As you meditate ask questions about your purpose and how to fulfill it:

- What's yours to give in this lifetime?
- In what ways are you here to reveal more beauty, love, abundance, wellness, etc.?

Meditate often and keep a journal near by to record the messages that reveal themselves to you.

Create Your Own Special Goddess Meditation

- Using Frankincense and Clary Sage essential oils when meditating can be a baseline ritual that gets your mind and body ready.
- Frankincense is the oil of truth which can be placed on your third eye.
- Clary Sage is excellent at activating intuition, which is placed over the throat chakra.
- Melaleuca or Tea Tree Oil, is energetically the oil of boundaries. This helps to establish a safe container, where the information coming in, is of the highest vibration of love and light.
- For your Goddess Meditation, there are a few more oils. The first is Magnolia. This is a flowery oil. It's the oil of compassion that will help connect to the goddess energy. This is lovely on your heart chakra.

- Myrrh, is the oil of Mother Earth. It's very important to stay grounded to Mother Earth.
- Lastly, Petitgrain, which is the oil of ancestry. It's so important to honor all of the women, matriarchs, and all of the divine women that came before us.

When Essential Oils are incorporated into the practice of meditation, they can help to center, ground, and focus the mind and are said to help eliminate or reduce negative energy and self-talk from the body and mind by encouraging insightful, elevating feelings of positivity, determination, optimism, gratitude, and self-respect. Furthermore, Essential Oils are reputed to ease, calm, and soothe the body. For higher purposes, such as meditation, it is recommended that only the highest quality oils be used in order to derive the most beneficial therapeutic effects.

Applying essential oils on your skin topically has been known to have healing effects on a myriad of different health problems. Essential oil comes from plants, so it makes sense that the direct oil from the plants containing these healing properties will have a positive effect.

It is important to know that pure essential oils are very potent. It is recommended, almost mandatory, to dilute the essential oils through some kind of oil like coconut, avocado oil or almond oil. The plant oil is potent when not diluted and can cause harmful reactions with your skin if applied undiluted.

Topical Application: If applying oils directly to the skin, ensure that they are diluted first. A few drops can be diluted in a Carrier Oil and the blend can be rubbed on the pulse points, such as the wrist and inner elbow. Those who believe in a third eye can dab a small amount onto this area and massage it into the skin. If there are any sore areas of the body, Essential Oils may be applied to these areas to help redirect the mind way from focusing on the bodily discomfort and to enhance mental focus on meditation. You can dab a drop onto pulse points like your temples and wrists, or delicate areas, behind the ears and on the throat and other chakra locations. Diluted Essential Oils may also be rubbed into the palms for inhalation.

Diffuser or Room Spray: For an ambient atmosphere that inspires improved focus and invigorates the senses, the chosen Essential Oils can be diffused or they can be diluted in a spray bottle of water to create a room spray.

Start meditating by just focusing on your breath and breathing in the aroma of all the divine essential oils you choose to use. Breathe deeply for maximum benefit, and let the comforting and restorative properties of essential oils compliment your spiritual practice.

Examine Your Beliefs

Beliefs are about:

- How we think things really are,
- What we think is really true and
- What we therefore expect as likely consequences that will follow from our behavior.

You become what you believe you are. Think of yourself as a work in progress. Actually, we all are. As we gain more knowledge and experience we sometimes change our minds, our opinions and our beliefs. And that's ok. It's called maturing. Maturing is gaining experience. So it is natural to change your opinions and beliefs as you go through life.

Change Your Beliefs and You Change Your Life

Researchers of two American Universities found that your beliefs have a direct impact on your body and health, because your beliefs actually alter your body's chemical balance. It means that what you regularly think has a direct impact on your health and your body. Because what you regularly think is what you end up believing.

Change the way you think, you change your beliefs and you change your life and the way you live it. Yes you can actually improve your life and your body by having a positive attitude and a positive belief system. With positivity in place you'll live a healthier, longer life.

Many of the limitations you face in life are self-imposed. What you believe about yourself can keep you locked behind your fears or thrust you forward into living your dreams.

Make a list of your core beliefs. Take an inventory.

- What do you believe?
- What beliefs have been handed down to you that don't feel right to you?
- Which beliefs bring you joy?
- Which ones cause you fear?
- Which ones do you want to release?
- Which ones do you want to keep?
- What do you want to believe in?

Identify and get rid of old limiting beliefs that may be holding you back. We all pick up limiting, false beliefs along the way which keeps us from being all we can be. Those beliefs can even cause pain and suffering. Resolve to really look at the things you believe in and WHY you have the belief.

Realize that no one is forcing you to believe anything and that beliefs are not a part of who you really are. Determine to keep an open mind and know that limiting beliefs may be keeping you from fully connecting with your Inner Goddess. Clearly see that false beliefs can restrict you from experiencing all the goodness of life, as well as contributes to suffering and a sense of struggle in life. Determine to let them go!

An open minded person will consider all opinions and have a greater chance of finding the truth. A closed minded person will only believe their own interpretation of life and never consider a different opinion.

As we mature and learn we usually change our mind on many things which we once thought to be true. It is normal if we continue to grow, we let go of old beliefs we no longer believe in.

Once you identify old beliefs or old roles that you want to change, have a fire ceremony and release them forever to the universe.

Burning Old Roles and Identities, as taught by Dr. Alberto Villoldo

The micro-fire ritual is an effective practice for rewriting the brain and shedding outworn roles and identities, so you can release the constraints of the past and move on. It requires focusing your intent on the task. It is your intent that gives the ritual depth, significance, and the transformative power. Remember that the ancient limbic brain changes through the power of ritual.

Traditionally, this ritual involves a group of people gathered around a large fire outdoors, but it can be just as meaningful as a solo rite indoors.

You will need a fat candle, at least four inches tall, a box of wooden toothpicks, matches, and fireproof bowl. You can fill the bowl part way with sand, if you would like.

Light the candle, and then pick up the toothpick. As you hold it, think of a role or identity that is no longer serving you. Blow gently into the toothpick, envisioning that you are transferring all the feelings of that outmoded role or identity into the small piece of wood. Then hold the toothpick to the candle flame. When you can no longer comfortably hang on to the flaming stick, drop it into the bowl. Continue blowing roles and identities into the toothpicks, on by one, until you have burned up all the stale old roles and identities you need to release.

It is Time to Question Everything

Voltaire said 'Judge a man by his questions
rather than by his answers.'

People get incredibly complacent and trusting in established beliefs and theories, therefore consider it beyond their place to question logic that has been established by those who are seen as being more intelligent or enlightened. But if the shoes don't fit, don't be afraid to return them! It's wise to question, learn, grow, have your own opinion and change your mind if you are inspired to do so.

You have the right to question anything you feel the need to, passionately.

When you hear something that doesn't sound right or ring true, you need to pay attention to that feeling and question it. It is your intuition, your Inner Goddess, speaking to you.

A creative person is by nature a questioner. They are driven by doubt, curiosity and wonderment. It is our questions that fuel and drive our thinking. Many problems arise from making assumptions. If you assume, you think you know, when you probably don't. Questioning destroys assumptions.

If we were encouraged to maintain a child-like curiosity into our adult years we'd all grow up with a far better understanding of just how important it is to question why we do what we do and believe what we believe, which could potentially increase our happiness.

Why is it that the United States is the most prosperous country in the world, yet, is the leading country in mental illness? The two leading mental illness are anxiety and depression. Why is it that the U.S. has two times more people with anxiety and depression than any war-torn country and three times that of Africa?

When a lot of people are becoming mentally ill that tells us we aren't doing something right. People who chase affluence and wealth get mentally ill more than others. They have lost their balance of the real meaning of life.

Women are constantly bombarded with advertising concerning her beauty, weight and success. Today we are told to achieve more, be more, do more and buy more. If by the age of 30 you haven't made a career for yourself or opened your own business you are a failure.

Were you taught that if you were a nice, cute and lovable girl, you would and be loved and adored and swept off your feet by prince charming? Then why isn't it working? This is one of those old stories we need to let go of and stop teaching it to the upcoming generations of Divine Feminine girls.

Is This Really Progress?

We think we have made progress living in big cities and comfortable homes, driving outrageous automobiles that can take us hundreds of miles in no time, eating in restaurants and shopping in grocery stores without a thought of how or where the food is coming from, who sewed the clothes or who dug for the diamonds. But have we really progressed?

We are definitely more comfortable and acquiring necessities is more convenient. But our world is full of loneliness and depression. We are selfish and self centered, we barely know our neighbors or talk to our families. We are emotionally immature and our morality is in question.

Our obsession with technological innovation and our infatuation with electronic connectivity cuts us off from the web of life-force energy. Even with our cell phones and social media we feel isolated, invisible, lonely, disconnected and depressed. We eat artificial food, live with artificial light, breath recycled air, and suffer with insomnia.

Questioning why you do everything;

- forces you to pick apart the usefulness of habitual behaviors
- and to clarify aspects of your life
- and who you think you are, almost like a daily mid-life crisis.

A lot of people claim to want to know truth but do not practice the necessary rituals to do so. One of the most crippling aspects to identifying truth is bias/prejudice. Once you eliminate your bias on things it allows for the emotional and psychological barriers to be lowered, thus allowing us to accept and find full truth.

Ask questions of yourself constantly.
Ask yourself these questions:

- Why?
- Why not?
- Why not me?
- Why not now?

You can learn more by looking for an answer than finding it. Questions are more important than answers because they help you to be more engaged with the world around you.

Buddha said, "Believe nothing, no matter where you read it, or who said it, if I have said it, unless it agrees with your own common reason and common sense." He is telling his people to use their own experience as to who they have found to be insightful, reliable and wise and use their common sense as guides. Not all of the wise will agree, so you are going to have to figure things out for yourself ultimately.

CHAPTER 2

Feminine Rewilding

"Connecting with our ancient selves is a medicine that can heal us in this modern day. To allow our wild spirit to run free is the magic potion that many of us are missing. Embrace your ancient wild nature." Wild Woman Sisterhood

Remember the sassy, spunky, fun, sexy, spontaneous version of yourself? Have you lost touch with her? Most of us have. The good news is that she's still in there and she can't wait to be acknowledged! When I talk about wild, I'm talking about our natural state of being, the way we were before our modern culture changed us, labeled us, and confined us to unfitting ideals.

When ecosystems are depleted of resources, plant and wildlife growth is stunted, depleted, and many species go extinct. When we are cut off from our natural resources; the things we love, the things that make us feel alive, and the things that nourish us, our growth is stunted as well. Our intuition and creativity become stifled. Our instincts go unused. We are tamed into doing what our family thinks we should do, what society tells us to do, and convinced to consume things we don't need.

This form of taming causes us to feel depleted, unseen, disconnected, and highly vulnerable to traps. Most commonly, traps come in the form of the wrong jobs, the wrong relationships, the wrong ventures. These traps create lifestyles that only perpetuate our taming, a route nowhere in the vicinity of our wild self or true north. Discover your true north. Ask yourself who you are outside of the labels that social groups attach to you. Write down your personal values and how they guide your decisions in life as well as your lifestyle.

Pressures of domestication condition us to behave a certain way, look a certain way, and think a certain way. Each of these restrictions fulfill someone else's ideals and desires about who we should be and what role we should play in the world. We quickly forget that in order for nature to thrive, it needs earth, air, wind, water, fire, and sustenance; the things that make us feel grounded, alive, free, cleansed, renewed, and nourished.

Rewilding is answering the primal call to unapologetically be our true selves. It's about rekindling our instincts, that inner knowing of who to trust, what is right and wrong, where to go next, when to rest, pause, run, or hold strong. It's about knowing how to truly feed ourselves, literally and soulfully. It's a way of connected, authentic living.

Moving through life motivated by the primal senses of: desire, impulse and intuition, is one of the most powerful ways you can rewild your own life, wherever you currently are, without actually having to change very much in your external environment. Reclaiming this part of your sacred self is a potent way to reconnect with your Inner Goddess.

Spiritual Rewilding

Soulful rituals and habits are the undercurrents that drive your spiritual life. But they lose their potency when they become too perfect and neat, predictable and clean, sanitized beyond their original potency. Rewilding your spiritual life simply means loosening your grip on how you think your spiritual life should look to allow space for your heart to guide you by how it wants it to feel. Focus on the feeling. Unravel what you've been told a spiritual life is meant to be all about, and let your Inner Goddess guide you. Try new things. Have fun bringing new, spontaneous, joyful rituals and delicious, soulful ideas into your life that they take over with their wild, lush, overgrowth as you sink into this new way of being.

Fluid Rituals

If you're struggling to meditate in the morning, then move your practice to the evening, or at lunchtime in the park. If you keep forgetting to journal at night, put your journal next to your bed and jot down your thoughts in the morning, or take it with you so you have the opportunity to write your heart out during unexpected delays. There are no rules that say when you have to try your rituals. You don't need to put your crystals out on every full moon. You don't need to sage your house on every new moon. You don't have to love yoga... ever! Do what feels right, when it feels right for you.

Intuitive Direction

Your heart is guiding you every moment of the day. Move with this feeling. Your Inner Goddess loves to live wild in the world, not constricted inside a box. She wants to feel free to follow guidance straight from Source without your old beliefs or fears restricting her. Maybe that means sleeping naked or eating outside more, making your own drum or learning from a shamanic healer, chanting with sisters or adventuring in Mother Nature's raw wilderness. Start small if you need to, but learn to live wild.

Create Something Magnificent

If you can't find what you're looking for, you have the magic within you to create whatever it is you need. Start your own women's circle, online support group, soulful mastermind, healing collective, spiritual business, coaching service, or whatever is missing in your life that you cannot find elsewhere. Set a strong intention for how you want to feel, who you wish to work with and those you desire to serve.

Explore What Brings Excitement Into Your Life and Do More Of It

This could be giving back to your community, spending more time unplugging in nature, or picking up an old hobby you loved but no longer have time for. Make time for it and do more of it.

Disconnect and Remove What Doesn't Bring You Excitement and Happiness In Your Life

You only get one ride on the carousel of this life and getting off is the end of it. If negative relationships, feelings or commitments in your schedule are getting you down every time they come around, consider removing them and make way for more happiness.

Nourish Yourself and Your Body Through Routine Self-Care Rituals

Whether it's spending more time at the gym creating positive vibes and endorphins or soaking in a hot tub to relax and decompress, making time for yourself to unwind and relax is essential to coming home to your wild self.

Physical Rewilding

Carl Jung once said, "Whenever we touch nature we get clean." He, of course, did not mean clean in some sort of sanitary sense. He meant we get real and disinfect all of those extra layers of armor that modern life tames us with.

Rewilding is the process of undoing unhealthy modern conditioning and recreating cultures and lifestyles beyond domestication as we define it today. It is the process of rekindling our connection to nature and unearthing a truer, wilder, more holistic way of life that centers nature and simple living. Physical rewilding in essence means "returning to the basics" especially in living with the rhythms and seasons of nature. In some ways, rewilding mirrors many of the concepts of slow living to allow your body to experience nature as your rhythm guide.

Weekend Retreat

There's no denying how therapeutic it is to escape into nature and recalibrate. Treat yourself to a whole weekend of rewilding. Plan on going somewhere "away from the things of man". Plan to hike a long trail and camp along the way. Find a friend with a boat and experience a day or two out on the water.

Somewhere between learning to walk and learning to live, we forgot how to wander and meander.

Sounds of Nature

The sounds of nature have a rhythm that's stress relieving and soothing to our bodies. Some sounds of nature that you can seek out to rewild and de-stress:

- Bird sounds
- Frog croaks
- Cricket chirps

- Rain falling
- Brook babbling
- Ocean roaring
- Wind blowing through trees

Grounding

Go out in your front yard, your back yard, or whatever green space you have available to you, sans shoes. Have a little barefoot walk around, for just a few minutes, a half hour would be even better.

The pressure points of your feet are stimulated as you walk over uneven terrain. This is like nature's little foot massage or acupressure. This stimulates your root chakra, which is said to enhance feelings of security and groundedness.

Move Your Body

Run, dance, stretch, breathe deeply, and embrace your physical sensuality. Use your body to play and thrive inside that wild skin of yours.

Cool Baths

Our ancestors didn't have access to hot showers and bubble baths, but you don't have to go out and find a lake or stream to bathe in. You can rewild in your own shower simply by turning on the cold setting. If you can't imagine waking up in the morning to a splash of cold, try ending your regular hot shower with a couple of minutes of cold water before you get out. Cool water bathing is said to:

- Reduce cortisol
- Stimulate the immune system
- Tighten and firm skin
- Reduce itchy skin

Living In Natural Lighting

The Circadian Rhythm is your body's 24 hour clock, governing all the chemicals and processes in your body. When running smoothly, it helps you to be sleepy at night. And then it helps you to awake refreshed in the morning. It regulates the hormones that are behind all of your body's involuntary processes.

Unfortunately, modern electricity, as convenient as it is, has messed up a lot about our circadian rhythms. The availability of lights on at night helps us to ignore those feelings of sleepiness that come on after sundown. Instead of winding down, we're usually winding up for the night. As we stay up late under the lights in our home, our bodies' circadian rhythm signals become unbalanced. Many modern hormonal imbalances are tied to not getting to sleep early in the evening and not waking up with the sun.

Get up early like a Goddess and watch the sun rise. There is something magical and transformative about watching the light slowly fade on for a change, rather than fade off in the sunset. Make sure your natural lighting rituals include morning sunrise gazes.

In the evening walk outside and gaze at the moon. If I asked you what moon phase we're in right now, you'd probably have to google it. Our ancestors lived by the phases of the moon. Women's cycles have been historically linked to the moon. Today we're so disconnected from the moon because of electricity. Get back in touch with the phases of the moon by going out to look for it, or the lack of it, each night.

Eating in Season

Your body was designed to crave certain fuel at certain times of the year. As it turns out, your body doesn't just crave watermelon in the summer because of societal things like picnics and barbecues. Your body craves it because it's hydrating and summer is dehydrating. You naturally crave hot food and soups with starchy vegetables to keep warm in cold weather. Therein lies the genius behind giving your body whatever is growing in your region at any given time. Each season provides a variety of different crops to feast upon. Seasonal eating helps us learn the life cycles of edible plants and gives us an opportunity to revel in the deliciousness of each unique crop. Not only does this offer nourishment, but sourcing our food this way also helps us reduce our carbon footprint because crops don't have to travel great distances to reach our plates.

There's so much deep contentment to be found in eating simply, wasting as little as possible and spending time close to the earth, as well as supporting small local farmers.

Celebrate the Seasonal Shifts Like the Solstice and Equinox

The seasonal markers in nature coincide with the solar wheel of the year, which includes four solar festivals and four seasonal festivals. Honoring these seasonal markers throughout the year is an amazing way to live seasonally and be more connected to nature, the world-view it represents is quite old.

The concept of life and time as an endless repeating cycle is evident in the literature, art, and architecture of many ancient civilizations. Whatever names the feasts and celebrations were known as in the past, now long lost, helped them remain balanced in an uncertain world. The seasons changed, people died, but nothing was ever finally lost because everything returned again, in one way or the other, in a repeating natural cycle.

Once Christianity had triumphed over the pagan beliefs, their holy days of the year became Christianized. Yule became Christmas, Ostara became Easter, All Souls Eve became Halloween, and others renamed and associated with various saints.

Gather around a bonfire with friends and family for a seasonal feast and plenty of good stories to share. Each of these eight seasonal markers give us an opportunity to pause, notice the changes in nature, and embrace the season at hand.

Enjoy Your Senses

There is much talk about enhanced levels of spiritual awakening but the truth is, we are human beings having an embodied human experience. So to deny this is to deny a huge part of life and risks rejecting so much learning, healing and pleasure that comes through the body. The easiest way to begin to do this is to consciously connect to your life through the senses; to see, touch, taste, smell and listen to life.

CHAPTER 3

Know Thyself

"Knowing yourself is the beginning
of all wisdom" Aristotle

A woman armed with love and ancestral wisdom is an unstoppable force. When you tap into the Divine Feminine, you will awaken to new possibilities and birth a greater level of creativity in your life. By channeling your Inner Goddess, your relationships will become more loving and nurturing. You will experience a deeper sense of personal freedom and self-love. In no uncertain terms, you will have a spiritual awakening.

This sacred energy already exists within you. All you have to do is look within and you will find it there.

Knowing who you are, a divine being, a unique soul, a descendant of the first sacred women who lived on earth, should awaken your mind to connect with your spiritual heritage. You should feel proud and honored to be a descendant of such great and gifted beings.

Knowing who you are spiritually gives you knowledge and power to overcome the fears which hinders your ability to be all you can be while on this earth. You are a wise soul whose time has come to be on earth at this time.

Before you came to earth you had a plan for the things you wanted to accomplish on your life journey, what you wanted to learn and contribute to humanity. You came with a purpose and a mission to fulfill. No matter which profession or lifestyle you choose, your age or looks or ethnicity, you are divine, you are special, you are sacred, you are intuitive and wise beyond belief.

Feelings

Feel your feelings, don't be afraid of them. Feelings are a part of the grand experience of being human. They are also a part of our intuitive guiding system. The Divine Feminine feels deeply.

Interests

Know what interests you. "Interests" include your passions, hobbies, and anything that draws your attention over a sustained period of time. To figure out your interests, ask yourself these questions:

- What do you pay attention to?
- What are you curious about?
- What concerns you?

The focused mental state of being interested in something makes life vivid and may give you clues to your deepest passions. When you know what your passions are you will find your purpose.

Strengths

Know your strengths. "Strengths" can include not only abilities, skills, and talents, but also character strengths such as loyalty, respect for others, love of learning, emotional intelligence, fairness, and more. Knowing your strengths is one of the foundations of self-confidence; not being able to acknowledge your own superpowers could put you on the path to low self-esteem.

Temperament:

"Temperament" describes your inborn preferences.

- Do you restore your energy from being alone (introvert) or from being with people (extrovert)?
- Are you a planner or go-with-the-flow type of person?
- Do you make decisions more on the basis of feelings or thoughts or facts?
- Do you prefer details or big ideas?

Knowing the answers to temperament questions like these could help you gravitate toward situations in which you could flourish and avoid situations in which you could wilt.

Biorhythms

Know your biorhythms. Are you a morning person or a night person, for example? At what time of day does your energy peak? If you schedule activities when you are at your best, you are respecting your innate biology.

Your Baggage

At its simplest, emotional baggage is the sum of all the negative experiences you've had in relationships (both romantic and otherwise) that you bring with you throughout life. Know what baggage you are carrying around with you. While you can't really stomp out your emotional baggage for good (memories and experiences are forever, after all), there are ways to cope with how you're feeling and techniques for how to successfully keep emotional baggage from controlling your life and ruining your relationships. The first step to dealing with your emotional baggage is to admit that it does exist.

You may realize that an event caused you a good deal of pain. However, you have to come to terms that the event is over with. It's finished. The only amount of power it holds over you is the power you give to it. You need to take back that power. These events or situations are in the past. They hold no more power over you than you give them.

Acknowledge and Embrace Your Imperfections

At some point on your spiritual journey to unleash your Inner Goddess you will want to address your dark side. We all have one, it is the human condition. When we acknowledge our perceived imperfections we can do something about them, or not. But we must know our whole selves if we wish to make changes in our lives and belief systems.

A Divine Feminine is not perfect but she "owns" who she is, she is truthful with herself and others. She is also non judgmental and more accepting of others imperfections when she can recognize her own. When we struggle with understanding our imperfections and shun them, it tends to undermine and sabotage our lives.

Addictions, low self-esteem, mental illness, and chronic illnesses, may present themselves. When our emotions are suppressed or repressed in the unconscious long enough, they can even overtake our entire lives and cause extreme forms of behavior like cheating on one's partner or physically or emotionally harming others. Intoxicants such as alcohol and drugs also have a tendency to show up when we believe we are damaged goods or unworthy because of our short comings.

Both religion and modern spirituality have a tendency to focus on the "love and light" aspects of spiritual growth to their own doom. This over-emphasis on the fluffy, transcendental, and feel-good elements of spiritual progression can result in shallowness and naivete, living life with our head in the clouds or the opposite happens and we live with guilt, frustration, resentment and/or shame, believing we don't measure up to what is expected of us.

When we are born, we are full of potential, with the ability to survive and develop in a variety of ways. As time goes on, we learn more and more to become a certain type of person. Slowly, due to our circumstances and preferences, we begin to adopt certain character traits and reject others. For example, if we are born into a family that shows little interpersonal warmth, we will develop personality traits that make us self-sufficient and perhaps standoffish or mind-oriented. If we are born into a family that rewards compliance and shuns rebellion, we will learn that being submissive works, and thus adopt that as part of our personality.

What has happened to all those parts of our original potential that we didn't develop? They won't just cease to exist: they will still be there, as potential or as partly developed, then rejected, personality attributes, and they will live on in the unconscious.

There are countless behaviors, emotions, and beliefs that are rejected in society, and thus, are rejected by ourselves. In order to fit in, be accepted, approved, and loved, we learned to act a certain way. We adopted a role that would ensure our mental, emotional, and physical survival. But at the same time, wearing a mask has consequences. What happened to all the authentic, wild, socially taboo or challenging parts of ourselves?

Golden Shadow

What is the Golden Shadow? Carl Jung once stated that "the shadow is ninety percent pure gold." What this means is that there are many beautiful gifts offered to us by our Shadow side if we take the time to look. For example, so much of our creative potential is submerged within our subconscious because we were taught to reject it.

The 'Golden Shadow' also presents us with the opportunity for tremendous psychological and spiritual growth. By doing inner work, we learn that every single emotion and wound that we possess has a gift to share with us. Every spiritual path needs inner perspective and releasing trapped emotions that don't serve us well.

When you embrace your own radiance fully, in spite of any imperfections or shortcomings you believe you have, you'll become liberated from the fears that so commonly hold us back from expressing our power and allowing our divine feminine brilliance to shine.

To move forward and be successful you must really know yourself and unconditionally love yourself and forgive yourself, just as you try to accept, love and forgive others. As they say, when you own who you are, no one else can hold it against you.

You Have To Know Yourself To Be Yourself

For all of us, being yourself sounds easier than it actually is. Who are you at your core? What most matters to you, what makes you come alive, what feeds your soul and what drains your spirit? When you're by yourself there's nobody around to impress;

no one to analyze. It's just you. And because of that, you don't focus on yourself, but on what you're doing. Shut down your inner clamoring for approval and focus on being present in the external world. You'll have a lot more fun.

Being yourself makes you special. Think of what the word special means; unique, different, or even precious. By being special you are one of a kind, you stand out in a crowd, and honestly it makes you much less of a boring person because you have so many different thoughts and ideas compared to everyone else. If people weren't different from one another who would set trends, have new creative ideas, or even change the world?

Be True To Yourself

Being authentic frees you from the chains of other people's perceptions of you. You'll feel freer and stronger because you no longer conform to how you "should" feel, think, or act. For example, I can remember my relief when I realized I was naturally an introvert. How comforting it was to finally give myself the gift of time alone without wondering or worrying that I was anti-social.

As difficult as it may seem at first, have the courage to accept yourself as you really are, not as someone else thinks you should be. Do not take action or pretend to be someone else for the sake of gaining acceptance.

You don't owe a thing to other people's opinions. They no longer matter. Self-respect comes from being true to who you really are and from acting in accordance with your fundamental nature.

When you respect yourself, others will respect you. They will sense that you are strong and capable of standing up for yourself and your beliefs.

When you are true to yourself, you allow your individuality

and uniqueness to shine through. You respect the opinions of others but do not conform to stereotypes or their expectations of you.

Tips On Being True to Yourself

- Be who you are, be your genuine Divine Feminine self
- Follow your own value system and common sense
- Listen to the advice of others, but make up your own mind
- Recognize, appreciate, and develop your unique talents
- Stand up for what you believe in
- Know that being 'different' is a gift

CHAPTER 4

Divine Personal Development

*"There will be very painful moments in your life
that will change your entire world in a matter
of minutes. These moments will change you. Let
them make you stronger, smarter, and kinder.
But don't you go and become someone you
are not. Cry. Scream if you have to. Then you
straighten up your crown and keep moving."*

12 Steps For The Divine Feminine

1. If it feels wrong, don't do it.
2. Say exactly what you mean.
3. Don't be a people pleaser.
4. Trust your instincts.
5. Never speak bad about yourself.
6. Never give up on your dreams.
7. Don't be afraid to say no.
8. Don't be afraid to say yes.
9. Be kind to yourself.
10. Let go of what you can't control.

11. Stay away from drama and negativity.
12. Love.

Think and Act Like a Goddess

You are a Divine Feminine and you have an Inner Goddess, she is a part of you. She is within you. So start acting like it! This means creating a healthy life for yourself; no more bad habits, toxic relationships, or fear. More self-love, good decisions and healthy habits! When faced with tough decisions, ask yourself, what would a Goddess do? Remember, goddesses aren't always love and light. Sometimes they have to stand up and fight, in these instances, invoke the warrior goddesses.

Living From Your Heart

The heart is the largest generator and receiver of electromagnetic energy in the body. The electromagnetic field of the heart is 5,000 times greater than the brain. It can be measured 10 feet away from the body. The heart field is the reason why we can feel the energy of other people, plants and animals. If you are an empath you can feel the emotions of other people, like a radio receiver. When we tune into the heart field we can pick up energetic qualities bringing on a whole new level of profound. When you feel with your heart more you become more present, focused, intuitive and empathic.

Listen to your heart more often. Take 5 minutes to close your eyes and listen to your heart beat every now and then. You will become a more calm and receptive person. Empty your mind and open your heart. It's hard to learn when you think you already "know".

Living from your heart will become your guidance. On a spiritual level it is your "minds eye".

Prayer

- Regardless of spiritual or religious beliefs pray to any higher power you hold your faith in.
- Prayer helps you to be in better alignment with your path.
- Use prayer to call in faith, joy, a loving partner, etc.
- Use prayer to call in infuse intention into anything; food, craft, medicine, etc.
- Give thanks for family, friends, overcoming challenges, etc.

Sacred Space

Ritual and sacred ceremony used to be a way of life for women in ancient times. There was a greater sense of community amongst people, and women of all ages would regularly come together to converse, share, or celebrate; on new and full moons, while bleeding, and during seasonal celebrations.

Sacred ceremony and rituals act as a bridge between the two worlds: earth and the spirit. Your fears and anxieties and shadows are able to be met, and softened, with compassion and the great power of friendship between women.

The feminine within you craves to be in beautiful sacred spaces, that have been created with pure intention and love. Creating ritual and sacred space in your life can be simple;

- Lighting a candle before you meditate or practice yoga, or even take a bath.
- Making a sacred altar for yourself, however small or grand you like, with sacred objects that speak to you.
- Celebrating the new moon with releasing and intention setting; or the full moon by dancing and singing in the moonlight with gratefulness in your heart.
- Or perhaps you attend a women's circle near you, or you host your own.

Beautify Your Personal Space

Select a special area as your divine space. Adorn it with lovely things that you relish as the goddess, such as beautiful flowers, crystals, or lovely gentle goddess music or sounds. Mother Earth has so many gifts for you to enjoy.

Decorate your space in a way that allows a submersion into YOU. Everything that you choose to put your own beauty, energy, and truth into, is YOU.

What makes you feel good? Surround yourself with THAT.

Comfort in Self-Care Routines / Rituals

Having a routine and knowing what comes next is what gives you sanity. To be clear, a routine is not a schedule! It is doing things in a particular order consistently. Routines simplify your life and help you get things done and gives you a sense of purpose. They make you feel safe and comfortable. The world can be a chaotic and uncertain place, and a routine is predicable and certain. On a bad day sometimes a routine is all you have to hold on to. Routines are as helpful for you as they are to children and pets.

Routine becomes the pathway to flow, when we become so invested in what we are doing, all ideas and worries dissolve, and we're completely invested in the task.

Not having a routine can cause you to suffer from stress, poor sleep, poor eating and poor physical condition. I think a goddess would have her routines. We are each different so our routines will be different. The following are a few suggestions for incorporating self-care practices into your daily routines. Choose the ones you like and make your own.

- Push yourself to get up before the rest of the world, start with 7am, then 6am, then 5:30am. go to the nearest hill with a big coat and a scarf and watch the sun rise.

- Push yourself to fall asleep earlier, start with 11pm, then 10pm, then 9pm. wake up in the morning feeling re-energized and comfortable.
- Lie in your garden, feel the sunshine on your skin.
- Get into the habit of cooking yourself a beautiful breakfast. Sit and eat and do nothing else.
- Stretch. Start by reaching for the sky as hard as you can, then trying to touch your toes. Roll your head. Stretch your fingers. Stretch everything.
- Buy a 1L water bottle. Start with pushing yourself to drink the whole thing in a day, then try drinking it twice.
- Buy a beautiful diary and a beautiful black pen. Write down everything you do, including dinner dates, appointments, assignments, coffees, what you need to do that day. No detail is too small.
- Strip your bed of your sheets and empty your underwear draw into the washing machine. Wash, then hang them in the sunshine with care. Make your bed in full.
- Dig your fingers into the earth, plant a seed. See your success as it grows everyday.
- Organize your room. Fold all your clothes, bag what you don't want, clean your mirror, your laptop, vacuum the floor.
- Light a beautiful candle. Breathe. Practice your deep breathing. Ground yourself.
- Have a luxurious shower with your favorite music playing. Wash your hair, scrub your body, brush your teeth. Lather your whole body in moisturizer.
- Push yourself to go for a walk. Take your headphones. Smile at strangers walking the other way and be surprised how many smile back. Bring your dog and observe the dog's behavior. Realize you can learn from your dog.
- Think long and hard about what interests you. Find a book about it and read it.

- Become the person you would ideally fall in love with.
- Let cars merge into your lane when driving. Pay double for parking tickets and leave a second one in the machine.
- Compliment people on their cute clothes.
- Challenge yourself to not ridicule anyone for a whole day, then two, then a week.
- Walk with a straight posture.
- Look people in the eye. Ask people about their story. Talk to acquaintances so they become friends.
- Lie in the sunshine. Daydream about the life you would lead if failure wasn't a thing.
- Journaling
- Exercise
- Meditation
- Health and beauty rituals
- Reading, writing, hobbies
- Spending time with your partner
- 9 p. m. turn down the bright lights, use table lamps
- Watching the sun rise and set
- Moon rituals

Begin today to start treating yourself like the Goddess you are. Schedule the time you need for alone time and make it happen. The key lies not in finding time but creating time for yourself. The power is in your hands to control your time.

No two days are alike and we need to honor ourselves enough to include flexibility on our Goddess journey and learn to go with the flow rather than get frustrated when our best laid plans are occasionally interrupted.

Importance of Ceremonies, Celebrations & Traditions

Celebrations, traditions, ceremonies and rituals keep us engaged and interested in our life. Our ancestors knew this and used these practices to stay happy and energized, always having something to plan and look forward to right around the corner. They were much wiser than we give them credit for. In our modern chaotic, fast paced world we are too busy, too tired, too broke, self absorbed, disenchanted and disconnected from each other and rarely participate in traditional celebrations.

Ceremonies

Ceremonies are held to celebrate a new life or in honor of a life well lived, for a graduation or a retirement, for a marriage or commitment.

Communities hold ceremonies to reflect on events of historical and social significance and events that caused devastation or loss; ceremonies simply help to heal. A ceremony can help to show people they are united and they belong. Example: During a simple new school year ceremony, new teachers and students are welcomed and all are invited to place a pebble into the Community Bowl. A simple act with a great and powerful meaning. Each pebble represents one unique individual, the action saying you are welcome and you are a part of our group, you are a valuable member of our community.

Ritual and ceremony are deeply important to human beings. Some say that ritual is what makes us human. Done well, ritual and ceremony provide a sense of "before and after" and people come away knowing their lives have been positively touched by the experience. Ritual and ceremony make and mark change within a community of family and friends.

Traditions

Tradition contributes a sense of comfort and belonging. It brings families together and enables people to reconnect with friends. Tradition offers a chance to say "thank you" for the contribution that someone has made. Tradition serves as an avenue for creating lasting memories for our families and friends. Cultural traditions are important because they transmit shared values, stories and goals from one generation to the next. Traditions encourage groups of people to create and share a collective identity, which in turn serves to shape individual identities.

Celebrations

Celebrations throughout the year give us something fun to look forward to and prepare for. It breaks up the monotony of everyday life schedules and responsibilities which can leave us feeling isolated and disconnected from other human beings. Celebrations make life enjoyable and connect us to others in the world.

Celebrate the fact that you are alive. Take a few moments every morning to simply enjoy a few minutes over a cup of coffee, coco or tea and breathe in the aroma, feel the warmth, and enjoy the comfort. Give thanks for the day that is coming your way. When you begin your day with a sense of gratitude and celebration, you are bound to have more joy for the rest of the day.

Celebrate yourself. All too often we take our divine selves for granted. If you find you are taking yourself for granted start taking notice of all the awesome things you do on a daily basis. When we notice the little things in life that we do well, it improves our mood and self esteem. Did you use your lunch break taking a walk and getting some exercise to take care of your body? Did you spend a few extra minutes giving your friend or co-worker a helping hand to make their life a little easier? Give yourself the credit you deserve for being the awesome Divine Feminine that you are.

Sometimes acknowledgment of our deeds and successes is sufficient, other times may call for more self-love like taking yourself for a pedicure, or dinner with friends or a weekend getaway. You may not be able to celebrate big all of the time but when you can it is healthy to celebrate yourself in luxury. Treat yourself like the Divine Feminine you are. Every now and then open that bottle of champagne or sparkling cider and celebrate a job well done, a fantastic week or a huge project accomplished.

Feminine Creativity

Masculine energy is destructive energy, while feminine energy is a creative energy.

The Divine Feminine in all of us is associated with creative energy and life force energy. Similar to the energy of flowing emotions or timelessness, the feminine craves creativity. Our wombs are designed to create life after all.

Creativity is the act of turning new and imaginative ideas into reality, to bring something into being that, without your heart and hands, would not otherwise exist.

Creativity is characterized by the ability to perceive the world in new ways, to find hidden patterns, to make connections between seemingly unrelated phenomena, and to generate solutions. Creativity involves two processes: thinking, then producing.

Some ways of expressing creativity are through crafting, painting, dancing, clothing, handiwork, photography, decorating, cooking, entertaining guests, writing, comedy or gardening. Expand your mind and see where in your life you are creating something out of nothing. It's a common misconception that traditional "art" is the only form of creativity!

It's not uncommon to feel down in the dumps from time

to time, especially during periods of hardship and transition. Thankfully, from simple doodling to singing your favorite song, moments of intentional creativity can come to the rescue, no matter your current lot in life. So shake things up in your routine and paint, create a poem, write a song, create perfume with essential oils, or make a delicious meal for yourself and others.

The song, poem, or meal doesn't even necessarily need to be "good" it just needs to be created. Let go of expectations and simply create for creations sake.

Things that excite you are not random. They are connected to your purpose. Follow them.

Being creative helps you become a better problem solver in all areas of your life and work. Instead of coming from a linear, logical approach, your creative side can approach a situation from all angles. Creativity helps you see things differently and better deal with uncertainty. Studies show that creative people are better able to live with uncertainty.

Being creative has many advantages. The first advantage that comes to mind is most creative people can entertain themselves. Creative activities have been shown to improve overall emotional health. Creativity increases our control over emotional pain and depression. This is due to the self-reflection and greater understanding of oneself that often comes with making something. You are connecting with yourself in a way that you couldn't otherwise. Socializing over creative acts promotes more than happiness; studies indicate it promotes health, too. So, make it a lifelong mission to take advantage of the socializing benefits of creative acts.

Let your Inner Goddess shine by expressing your thoughts and feelings through creative outlets. Creation is such a feminine concept and connecting to your creative self allows you to practice giving and receiving with the universe.

Find a new hobby, indulge in art or music, write a poem or story, anything that lets your true, authentic self sparkle.

Divine Beauty

- Beauty is grace.
- Beauty is love.
- Beauty is inner peace.
- Beauty is being comfortable in one's body.
- Beauty is glowing with all those things that make us glow.
- Beauty is loving yourself and caring for yourself and your body.
- Beauty is shinny hair, soft skin and womanly curves.
- Beauty is smelling nice.
- Beauty is multi-dimensional.

Some of us never had any sort of classic look which our culture considers beautiful. We don't all look like models or movie stars. Some women are plain, or large, or old, or born with afflictions, or simply don't give a damn what they look like because they're too busy saving the world or their children.

When we are young it is normal to compare ourselves to other girls and wish we had hair like theirs, bigger boobs, longer legs, a prettier face, etc. Power, strength and character are more important than physical beauty and always will be. The sooner we learn this the happier and more confident we will be in our own skin.

Too many pretty girls, shallowly, live off of their looks to get by and get what they want. But physical beauty fades over time. If you don't develop your character, talents or skills, you will end up unhappy with your life and your looks, as your youth fades away. You might also end up looking like plastic if you have too many procedures trying to stay looking young into your old age.

We just have to do the best we can with what we've got. Some women hit the genetic lottery and others don't. It is sometimes more of a blessing to not be born too beautiful. We are then forced to develop our character, sense of humor and intelligence.

For better or worse, we are not our bodies, our bodies are the vehicle for our soul to have an earthy experience. Some of us are given a high maintenance Rolls Royce, some get a Chevy, and most get something in between. Whatever we get, they all take us where we need to go and that's a beautiful thing. Be grateful for your vehicle, your Divine, miraculous, beautiful body.

You are valuable and important just as you are. Be yourself just as you are. You are enough just as you are. You are a beautiful, ageless Goddess inside your Divine Feminine body.

Everything Carries Frequency, Even Words

*"If the words you spoke appeared on your
skin, would you still be beautiful?"*

Every word carries an energy that can be sensed regardless of whether you speak it, think it, hear it or read it on a page. A word is more than it's definition because it contains energy and power.

Words have many layers and are more than just a way to communicate because words have energy, they hold a vibration. We feel good or bad vibes from certain words because there are positive energy and negative energy words.

Words vibrate at different frequencies which affect us. A good example is the word love. The word love vibrates at a much higher frequency than the word hate. You can feel the difference in the energy of the two words.

You can attract positive energy to you by using high vibrational words, a good example would be words used in meditation, chanting or during prayer.

Other positive energy words are words like love, inspiration, hope, joy, happiness and even a word like possibility has an expansive feeling to it. But you can use any words that raise your vibration, motivate you or light you up!

Perhaps the easiest way to begin to live an abundant life is by watching the words you use and making sure that the energy that fuels your words carries high vibration. You may never have thought about words holding a certain vibration but you most certainly have had the experience.

Since we can feel the difference between the energy of words, pay attention to how certain words make you feel and surround yourself with positive high-vibe words.

If you notice words you commonly use carry low vibrational energy, make a commitment to shift your words. Identify consistent phrases, or expressions and begin to rephrase them in order for them to represent a higher vibration. You might even be realizing words or phrases that you use consistently that need to be transformed, such as:

- "You should" becomes "It might serve you to"
- "I'm tired of you always" turns into "wouldn't it be nice if"

The words we use daily can affect our lives positively or negatively. Your words can be the building blocks as your Inner Goddess seeks to build an abundant Divine Feminine life.

Clear Your Head and Hold Your Tongue

Too many times we find ourselves lashing out at those around us for various reasons. It is unacceptable that we sometimes treat the people who love us and do the most for us, worse than we treat strangers, neighbors or casual acquaintances.

You may have unresolved issues that you haven't dealt with that come out at the most inappropriate times. Whatever the reason, from the heart the mouth speaks. If you have an underlying problem it's time to listen to it and clear your head.

It's not anyone elses fault that instead of dealing with the issue at hand you held it in and then exploded. It's not anyone elses fault that you are feeling overwhelmed. That isn't any excuse to behave badly. You are in control of your responses.

Words matter. If you abuse your words in the name of stress you will hurt yourself first and others secondly.

Be careful with misplaced anger. Instead of acting as if your feelings aren't valid, get quiet and deal with them. Take a time out and stop lashing out at those around you.

Your plate being full is not an okay reason to mistreat others, talk to others with nasty tones, or lash out. Take control and simply don't speak until you have something better to add to the conversation or situation.

Self-discipline begins with mastery of your thoughts. If you can't control what you think, you can't control what you say or do.

The biggest lie that can be told is the one that you tell yourself. You can't hide from yourself. You know yourself very well. You know your intentions even when you hide them. You know your triggers and you know how to control them, for the most part.

Take some quiet time for yourself each day. You may be very busy but you can make it happen. First thing in the morning before facing your day is a great time to talk to yourself, practice gratitude, pray, meditate, journal or whatever works for you to clear your head and set the intention to control your thoughts, actions and reactions to your life's daily situations.

A Goddess is in control of her actions and reactions. Remember who you are.

How to Apologize Like a Goddess

Apologies are not always easy, but that can be an important part of mending or maintaining important relationships. With empathy, an open heart, and a dose of courage, you can take the steps you need to make a sincere and honest apology.

1. Don't apologize for someone else's feelings.
   "I'm sorry you're mad" is not an apology. It's condescending.

2. Do apologize for your own actions and attitude.
   I'm sorry I was rude" is an apology that takes ownership. Be specific about what you did wrong. "I'm sorry for whatever made you mad" is not going to work.

3. Don't add an excuse to your apology.
   "I'm sorry I was rude, but I was really irritated", means you're not really sorry. You feel justified for the way you acted and you expect to be excused. Never say I'm sorry BUT......

4. It's important to be fair in your apology, both to the other person and to yourself. Don't accept all the blame if it isn't all your fault.

5. Do ask for forgiveness when you apologize.
   "I'm sorry" on it's own is just a statement. It requires no response. "Will you forgive me?" is a humble request that can build a relationship. Remember when you are in the wrong you are never owed forgiveness. Be grateful when you receive it.

6. Don't expect a reciprocal apology.
   Just own your own part of the wrong doing.

7. Do attempt to make a repair.
   It's wise and loving to ask "Is there anything I can do to make this right?"

8. Learn from your mistakes and find new ways of dealing with difficult situations. If you keep repeating the offense, you are not sorry.

Reasons why people don't apologize are:

- They aren't really concerned about the other person
- or apologizing threatens their own self-image,
- or they believe that an apology won't do any good anyway.

Not apologizing when you are wrong can be damaging to your personal and professional relationships. It can also lead to rumination, anger, resentment, and hostility that may only grow over time.

Take Your Pants Off

The Divine Feminine comes from many walks of life, different cultures and is many ages. Some of us are girly and some of us are tom boys, some like to cook and others like to climb mountains, some are artistic and others race cars. We all get to be who we are. Our personality isn't what makes us a Divine Feminine, it is our energy.

Divine Feminine Energy is receptive, soft fluid, intuitive, empathic, nurturing, emotional, flexible and sensual, expressed through our individual personalities.

Because feminine energy is pure motion and movement, it doesn't like to be boxed in or restricted. Jeans and pants have this restrictive tendency. Do an experiment and go on a "pants detox" and commit to only wearing skirts or dresses or tunics for a month.

See how you feel. Do you find it easier to flow through your life? Do you feel less restricted and more divine? Soft flowing fabrics mirror the constant moving element of feminine energy in a tangible way.

Get up 15 minutes earlier so you can take care of yourself and look your best so you feel your divine feminine best. Take a shower, moisturize your skin and get dressed every morning. Pick out pretty clothes, get a favorite lipstick color, wear your favorite jewelry, or buy a nice pair of pretty shoes.

Don't wait for a special occasion to get dressed up and wear your best clothes. Every day you are alive is a special occasion and clothes go out of style waiting to be worn.

Beauty is a woman's natural trait. When you start to allow feminine energy to flow back into your life, people will notice. In the past, I had a difficult time with compliments on my physical appearance. I would get embarrassed and brush them off. Now I smile warmly and say, "Thank you." Feel proud to be beautiful in someone else's eyes. Enjoy the compliments, they are simply a recognition that your divine feminine energy is flowing more freely than before. It means you're bringing your energies back into balance.

Connect to your femininity. Ask yourself these questions:

- What is femininity for you?
- When do you feel most feminine?
- What do you do on a daily basis to connect to your femininity?

Every day, put on something that makes you feel your "truth", your love for your Inner Goddess beauty inside and out. Jewelry, makeup, hair accessories, anything that makes you feel "I am a Goddess." It's all in the details, and confidence is key!

Divine Independence

Women have always been understandably concerned with their physical and safety needs. This is because we are the mothers, so we are constantly worried about how to obtain resources for our offspring and ourselves, also we are not the strongest physically, so safety is always a pressing matter for us. In ancient times we had help and protection in our tribes and clans. Then came marriage and separation from our extended families.

Social conditioning has ingrained in us to value one thing only; a man. From the time we are able to start processing the world around us we are bombarded by information and images that tell us that all we should concern ourselves with is how to get a man and how to keep him.

We were read fairytales and watched Disney movies which show amazing princesses who are unhappy until they find their handsome prince. The villains in the stories are jealous old hags without a man. And we see we should prioritize getting a man while we are young so we don't end up like the old ugly hag. As a result pursuing romantic relationships take up the majority of our time as young adults instead of cultivating our own personalities and chasing our own dreams while in the freedom of our youth.

We have our whole lives to be wives, mothers and caretakers, if that is what we wish, and there is no turning back once you go there. If you don't get an education, travel or develop desired skills or peruse personal interests while you have the time and freedom, you my never have the opportunity or at the very least will be difficult in the midst of family obligations.

The more life you have lived, places you've gone, friends you've made, hobbies you've tried, talents you've honed, not only fulfill you as a human being but you have something to add to conversations, it makes you more interesting to be around and attracts people of like mind and interests you would want to befriend.

It is a sad thing to see a woman who married young and began having children without ever having the opportunity to experience a life of her own. Then when her prince charming turns out to not be so charming, her bubble bursts and her dreams are shattered, leaving her bewildered with potentially a long hard life ahead of her.

If this is where you find yourself now, it's time to unleash your Inner Goddess, rewild yourself, claim your independence and love yourself and your family fiercely. This is a different path than you would have intentionally chosen but your Divine Feminine Energy and your Inner Goddess will guide you to a better path and a better life.

Whatever stage of life you are in, young, middle aged or old, remembering your divinity and individuality will help you embrace self-love and divine independence. Mastering yourself allows you to have some control of your life experience and live a more joyful life.

Turn Off the TV and Detoxify Your Mind

"What if I told you Television is the monster in your home, and it's called a program for a reason. Your television is nothing more than an electronic mind-altering device. It has been designed to psychology change the way you see reality."

When televisions were invented in the 50's it was light hearted entertainment and the family sat together and watched in their living rooms. The programs were uplifting, funny and entertaining. There was music, singing, dancing and costumes. Ordinary folks got to see things that up until then, were only available to the wealthy and those who lived in big cities.

Today the television and much of social media is used to brain wash the public, dumb us down and desensitize us to sell us ideas and products. There are no moral codes of ethics. News stations don't report honest news, they manipulate it according to their political agendas. Most of the so called entertainment is violent, perverse, mindless and a waste of time. Television, news and social media is used more for propaganda than entertainment or propaganda disguised as entertainment.

Today there are no consequences for straight out lies and slander, so people and groups lie and exaggerate to promote their agenda. Many times it is very hard to decipher the truth from lies and people pick the side they want to be true, without any research or education on the subject, except for what they learn on TV. They parrot the words they have heard others say and speak with conviction and authority without checking the facts.

TV land, politics and Hollywood are not real life or a reflection of real life for the majority of people. If you turned off your televisions and actually talked to your neighbors you would find the world isn't as hostile, unhappy, prejudice or racist as the news would have you believe. Most people are good, loving, well intentioned folks.

The television and internet cause sensory overload to our nervous systems. We are faced with more threat and fear stimuli in a week than our Paleolithic ancestors faced in a lifetime. They worried about one lion roaring at them, not the whole jungle turning against them at the same time.

Don't waste hours of your day in front of a box that is sucking the life and joy out of you. Adrenaline and cortisol will flood your cells causing inflammation. Your head will be filled with nonsense and your mind will be filled with fear that will leave you in a state of paralyzed confusion, despair and fatigue. Television distorts our understanding of reality, it's filled with beautiful people doing amazing things and having great adventures in every show.

Every hour you spend in front of the TV is another hour you're not making the most of your own life. You could be playing with your family, hanging out with friends or doing an activity you enjoy. Connection is one of the basic human needs we all have and it will never be fulfilled by your television set.

We live sedentary lives than ever before with most people having jobs behind a desk. We compound this problem when we go home and sit down in front of the TV, because the electrical activity in our muscles stop when we're sitting and our muscles atrophy.

Your children will imitate your lifestyle so any choices you make will be echoed in the generations that follow. It's time to stop watching the fake world on television and start living your divine life instead.

CHAPTER 5

Attributes of a Goddess

*Darling, you're a goddess, a badass
and you've totally got this.*

Remembering Your Divinity

Our Inner Goddess-self has mastered both the visible and invisible world, and we know we are closer to integrating her when we, too, have more or less mastered the visible world and begun to explore the invisible one.

Your very existence is proof of your worthiness and divinity. You are a daughter of a heavenly mother and father, who you made a contract with before you came to earth. You came with a plan, an agenda to accomplish in this lifetime. Your Inner Goddess remembers this plan, she whispers to you through your intuition, your meditations, passions and your dreams, to help you remember who you are and why you are here.

Don't forget you are striving to be a divine goddess, like your heavenly mother, a return to your true self. It is something you consider important in all aspects of your life. It doesn't mean you are perfect, perfect is over rated, you are human after all.

If you always remember who you are, a divine feminine, a goddess in training, you will stay true to your authentic self. You will love yourself, take care of yourself and flow through this life with class and purpose. You will not let the smallness of others take you off your course of following your dreams and purpose in this lifetime.

Following Your Intuition

Your rational mind can measure choices and be very practical in assessing a situation, but maybe there is another underlying feeling that you can't ignore. This feeling is beyond the logical mind and often difficult to explain. It is a knowing beyond reasoning or proof.

Intuition may feel like instinctual knowing, a flash of insight, or a knowledge that's deeper than words. Because you can't explain it in words you may tend to not act on it and caulk it up to just a passing thought or feeling.

That voice and gut feeling you get when you know something inside yourself, that is your Inner Goddess herself communicating with you! To learn to listen to her you have to trust that instinct. Don't question it! Your purest intuitions are never wrong, you have to follow them and let your Inner Goddess take over and guide you.

Self-Love

If I asked you to name all of the things you love, how long would it take you to name yourself?

Love is a Divine Feminine quality. The act of self-care is a feminine quality. Loving and nurturing yourself is a feminine quality all earthly goddesses need to embrace.

- Self-love is the act of learning how to love yourself and accept yourself unconditionally and without any reservation about how incredible you are.
- Self-love is believing in yourself.
- Self-love is the action you take to ensure you are being and accepting your authentic self by tending to your needs. You must prioritize self-love in order to complete any self-care activities that nurture your well-being.
- Self-love is honoring your intuition and trusting that it will guide you in the right direction.

Pay attention to what people say to you out of anger, they've been dying to tell you that. Love yourself enough to see it for what it is.

Self-Compassion

We grew up in the old energy, where social conditions were harsh, competitive, insecure, driven by ego. We were scolded, criticized and held up to impossible standards. We were brought up to ask for external approval consciously and unconsciously.

This deep seeded conditioning is hard to overcome and regrettably we may have passed it on to our children, being unaware and unenlightened as to the harm it can cause.

Once you pour unconditional love and compassion towards yourself, you'll able to bypass the self-sabotage and see a more accurate picture in your life, work and relationships.

Forgive all the "mistakes" you made in the past, without them you wouldn't be where you are now. Accept that wherever you are now, you are exactly where you need to be.

Playfulness

Your Inner Goddess self is extremely playful. She wants to be intrigued and aroused by beauty with all her senses. Have an appetite for creativity and pleasure and keep your playful fire burning. A really simple example; when you hug your partner, have a full-body hug, touch, smell, listen to his heart-beat and the sound of his breaths, feel and "taste" the vibration and connection in the air.

Infuse your playful and feminine spirit into all aspects of your work and life. Where in your life/work are you being too serious? Sure, you take the responsibilities of your career seriously, but nothing should be too serious to override your playfulness.

Unleash your playful self and enjoy your short time on earth, it's a gift meant to be enjoyed. Laugh a lot, belly laugh, laugh until you cry, laugh at yourself, laugh with your friends, laugh out loud at a funny movie.

Don't be self-conscious. Your Inner Goddess is free and wild and really doesn't care about other peoples opinions.

Playful Quotes

- "Life is for deep kisses, strange adventures and rambling conversations"
- "Kitchens were made for dancing"
- "A simple "hello" could lead to a million things"

Living Authentically

This phrase gets thrown around a lot, but what does it really mean? Living authentically involves honoring your truth and avoiding things like dishonesty, manipulation, or denial of your needs.

Instead of living according to what other people say or suggest you should do, you follow insight gained from personal experience and live according to the guidance of your heart.

You are also honest with yourself about your needs and desires. You respect the rights and needs of others, but you work to achieve your goals as only you can. You work to maximize your potential, not someone else's.

Listen to your own soul, too many people listen to the noise of the world instead of themselves. Deep inside, you know what you want, let no one decide for you.

As you stand in your authenticity, you give others permission to do the same. When you peel back all the masks, layers, roles you play, and everything you are not, you can reveal who you really are, that's authenticity.

When you stand in your truth, you vibrate at your home frequency, or true unique energy signature, that is unique to you and only you. The one thing you have that nobody else has is You. Your voice, your mind, your story, your vision. So write and draw and build and play and dance and live as only you can.

Goddesses Are Not Wishy Washy

"Hesitation only enlarges, magnifies the fear. Take action promptly. Be decisive." David J. Schwartz

Your Inner Goddess isn't a people pleaser, she knows what she wants for herself and goes after it!

Be decisive. Right or wrong just make a decision. The answers to your life's questions begin and end with you. You're the only person who knows what you truly want. So stop asking around. Stop saying "I don't know!" Turn inward. Start knowing.

Don't make decisions out of fear or thoughts of what might happen but rather what could and should happen. Sometimes there isn't a right or wrong choice, just a different one, with different experiences.

Do nothing and nothing happens. Life is about making decisions. Either you make them or they are made for you. Making decisions is a skill, one that can be learned, one that you can get better at.

Don't feel bad for making a decision about your own life that upsets other people. The more you love your decision the less you will need others to love it. They have their own life and they get to make their own decisions, your decisions are really none of their business.

Take your time for big decisions: Being decisive isn't just about making fast decisions. In fact, when it comes to big decisions, you should not rush into a decision. Decisions related to your career and relationships, should be carefully considered. They need to be clearly thought through. Do not let yourself be pressured into a big decision. Be decisive, by all means, but do not be rash especially when it comes to the big decisions.

Break big decisions down into small decisions: Making decisions can often seem intimidating because of the size of the decision. A great way to get over that is to break a big decision down into several small ones. The small decisions will be easier to figure out, and will add up to the big decision, this helping you achieve the decision you wanted all along.

Give yourself a time limit: Have you ever noticed how you often get things done at the last minute, especially when there's a specified deadline? It's a common habit, one most of us are familiar with. You might procrastinate getting the thing done, but then get it done in record time in order to meet the deadline. Why not take advantage of that? You can do this by setting a concrete deadline for making a decision. When you have a specified time limit, you will be more decisive as you'll know that you don't have all the time in the world. The time limit could be whatever you want, from a few minutes to a few days, just make sure that you don't take too long.

Procrastination wastes time. If you decide to do something, just get it done. Don't over think it. Decide what kind of life you really want, and then say no to everything that isn't that. Ask yourself; What would the Goddess do?

Choose Sacred Simplicity

When you choose simplicity,
peace and harmony follow

Earth is an adventurous place. We came here to have fun, conquer, learn and bring our divine wisdom for the betterment of the planet. Don't spend too much of your precious time devoted to earthly treasures, worldly praise, keeping up with the Joneses or caring about others opinions of your choices or lifestyle. In the end you will take all of your experiences, memories and stories with you to the next life and leave all worldly things behind. Live your life so that you are not bogged down in a prison of debt and possessions but rather create a life where you can enjoy all the worldly experiences, places and people, as much as possible while you are here.

Live simply so you can live more. Smaller house; more love in the home. Less stuff; more money in your pocket. Spend less; travel more. Fewer belongings equals less to clean, more free time, less debt and more play. It is those Divine Feminine who have enough but not too much who are the happiest.

People who live far below their means enjoy a freedom that people who busy themselves upgrading their lifestyles will never know. Unnecessary possessions are unnecessary burdens. You have to pay for them, take care of them, organize and store them. When you look at something in your home, remember, that it used to be money in the bank, so make sure before you buy anything new, you really need it or really love it.

The more you own the more enslaved you become. Are you

really living your divine authentic life or have you become trapped in consumerism? Are you a part of our culture who loves things and uses people?

Our culture has bred consumers and addicts. We want too much, buy too much and eat too much. It starts with children who are given too much. British research found that the average 10-year-old has 238 toys but plays with just 12 of them daily.

In our misguided desire to give our children everything we wish we had as a child, we are doing them a disservice. When you give children more possessions than they are mature enough to care for, it actually causes them stress and anxiety when they don't want to put all of their things away. You try to teach them responsibility, organization, respect for others space, and the value of the cost of the toys and things you give them, all of which is overwhelming to them. And you can forget about them being grateful. The kids who played in big boxes and banged pots with wooden spoons probably had more fun.

The best things in life are not things. Things have their place and serve their purpose, there are some things that make our life easier, and some things just make us happy or feel pretty. But in the big picture of life what gives us real joy are people, love, places we have been, stories we can tell, things we have seen and experienced, and what we have been able to contribute to the world. In the end, hopefully, our earthly life will be memories of all these things, not one big blur of work, exhaustion and paying bills.

The more in debt you are in the fewer choices you have, the harder it is to go back to school or move to a new location or change your career to something you love doing but may be a smaller income. Remember if you live above your means, a golden cage is still a cage.

Living simply doesn't necessarily mean stark or barren, unless that is your style. It means living in an uncluttered environment. It means everything has a place and everything is in it's place. If you have more than that and have to find places to stuff things or your space is cluttered because there is no place to put your things, then you have too many things. Your "dream home" is not filled with clutter.

Once you decide you want to live life more and do more than just collect things, you have to learn to say no. No to yourself, your partner, your children and gift givers who want to give you more things.

Here are some fun ideas of gifts to give and ask for that will bring joy rather than clutter:

- Movie passes
- Festival passes
- Manicures and pedicures
- Hair appointment certificate
- Massage gift certificate
- Amusement park passes
- Miniature golf passes
- Concert tickets
- Sporting event tickets
- Gift cards
- Itune credit
- Kindle books
- Babysitting services
- Pet sitting services
- House cleaning services
- Car wash passes
- Gas card

Instead of buying more unnecessary things here are some ideas to authentically live life and create lasting memories:

- Save the money for a big vacation
- Save money for your interests and hobbies
- Invest in your education

- Go to a Broadway show
- Go on a picnic
- Go to the beach
- Weekend getaway
- Go camping
- BBQ party with friends
- Go to a fine dining restaurant
- Take dance lessons
- Go to the county fair
- Family portrait session
- Ski trip
- Horseback riding
- Hiking
- Classes and lessons
- Go to a retreat

Making lifestyle changes is difficult for everyone. Scaling back and buying less doesn't mean denying yourself or going without or giving up things you love or that make you happy. But you don't want to be a hoarder or keep things you don't really need or want. Your home is your castle, your safe place in the world and it should be filled with peace and love not dust and clutter. You also want to free up some of your valuable time and the energy it takes to organize, clean and care for all of your "stuff". The less you have, the more time and freedom you have.

Ideas to free yourself and live with less:

- De-clutter your home to see what you really have.
- Clean out closets and drawers, garage, storage sheds, under the beds and anywhere else you store things and donate what you don't need or want anymore.
- Organize your kitchen and get rid of old pots and pans, gadgets you never use, old expired food and cooking spices.

- Clean out the linen closet and toss old sheets and towels that aren't being used and neatly fold what is left.
- Look at your decorating clutter; furniture, nic nacs, pillows, lamps, pictures and mirrors, etc. If you love it or need it then keep it, but remember you have to dust and clean it all. If it's a hand me down, outdated or you don't love it, donate it.
- If you have holiday decorations, as each holiday comes around go through the boxes and donate what you don't want and throw out what is broken etc. Neatly organize what you want to keep and label the boxes.
- If you are a crafter you may have really old craft supplies you will never use. Donate it to a school or shelter and put it to good use rather than taking up space in your home. Neatly organize and label what you are keeping.

Depending on how big your home is, how large your family is and how much stuff you have, will depend how long this process may take you. Just take it slow and easy but don't give up the process until you have touched everything you own, de-cluttered, organized and cleaned everything.

Listen to your favorite music, or motivational speaker or audio book while you are working. If you can't take a whole day, take half a day or half an hour at a time, even 15 minutes cleaning out one drawer will keep you on track. This will make you think twice before buying anything new to bring into your home!

I periodically go through this process one cupboard or closet at a time. Each time it gets easier to let go of more "stuff". Even though I may still like something, if it isn't necessary and I am tired of dusting it or storing it, I thank it for being in my life and send it on it's way to be useful or pretty for someone else.

And when I see pretty things in the store that I don't need, I admire it and let someone else take it home to dust! I can't take it with me when I die and I don't want to spend my divine life cleaning and dusting. I want to live and play and enjoy my life.

A simple home can still be beautiful and feel warm and welcoming. In fact it is more so when there isn't clutter and too much to look at in one space. A few nice things are much more appealing than a lot of cheap stuff scattered everywhere.

You Are a Goddess Not a Hoarder

Our earthly lives are short and pass quickly. It is important to get in all of the experiences we can, while we can. Being surrounded and burdened with too many worldly possessions distracts us from our true purpose. To fulfil your purpose for being here you need to be in the world but not of the world. Don't be robbed of your time and money by flashy modern consumerism.

Worldly trinkets, glitz, glamor, fame, pride, money, worldly acceptance and opinions of others can be enticing and lure us off our path and make us forget why we are here. All of that does not impress the goddess.

Divine Forgiveness

Divine forgiveness is essential for humanity to continue to move forward toward balance and love. For many years there has been much negativity, doubt, fear, corruption, manipulation, power, and self service that needs to be overcome and forgiven. This is going to take a long while to see transformation.

To be the change we must exercise our Divine Feminine Energy of forgiveness to those who are causing injustice in the world now and to their ancestors before them who have caused much pain and suffering. It is not our place to judge others or hold them accountable for their actions. It is our place and our purpose on earth at this time, as the Divine Feminine, to bring more divine love and forgiveness to the world to allow change to take place.

Getting another person to change his or her actions, behavior or words isn't the point of forgiveness. Think of forgiveness more as to how it can change your life, by bringing you peace, happiness, and emotional and spiritual healing. Forgiveness can take away the power the offending person continues to wield in your life.

Forgiveness is ultimately about freedom. When we need someone else to change in order for us to be OK, we are a prisoner. In the absence of forgiveness, we're shackled to anger and resentment, uncomfortably comfortable in our misbelief that non-forgiveness rights the wrongs of the past and keeps the other on the hook. And, that by holding onto that hook, there's still hope that we might get the empathy we crave, and the past might somehow feel OK.

When our attention is focused outward, on getting the other to give us something, so we can feel peace, we're effectively bleeding out not only our own power, but also our capacity for self-compassion. What we want from the other, the one we can't forgive, is most often, love. Forgiveness is ultimately about choosing to offer ourselves love, and with it, freedom.

- Forgiveness is about freeing up and putting to better use the energy that is being consumed by holding on to grudges, harboring resentments, and nursing old wounds.
- Forgiveness is about choosing serenity and happiness over righteous anger.
- Forgiveness is about realizing that anger and resentment don't serve you well.
- Forgiveness is about living in the present, which is where reality occurs.
- Forgive yourself for any of your own failings which led you to allow yourself to be placed in harm's way.

Choose to get along with the person who hurt you, even if you don't love or even like them, if it's in your best interest to do so. Developing empathy is a good place to start learning how to forgive.

"Forgiving others is essential for spiritual growth. Your experience of someone who has hurt you, while painful, is now nothing more than a thought or feeling that you carry around. These thoughts of resentment, anger, and hatred represent slow, debilitating energies that will dis-empower you if you continue to let these thoughts occupy space in your head. If you could release them, you would know more peace." Dr. Wayne Dyer

With un-forgiveness, time does not heal all wounds, in fact, time further worsens and infects emotional pain. If you're unforgiving, you might bring anger and bitterness into every relationship and new experience.

When we find it difficult to forgive, often it is because we are not living in the present, and instead, we assign more importance to the past.

There's good news for the grudge holders and revenge seekers of the world. With practice, most anyone can learn to be more forgiving. You don't have to be the world's most forgiving person. If you work at it, it takes the edge off the stress and ultimately that helps you feel better.

Realize forgiving others is a spiritual, supernatural exercise. We are all human, we do occasionally slip and retreat from our highest self into judgment, criticism, and condemnation.

What if I'm the one who needs forgiveness?

The first step is to honestly assess and acknowledge the wrongs you've done and how they have affected others. Avoid judging yourself too harshly.

A friend of mine is a good example. He was irresponsible, made poor choices, became an alcoholic and as a result lost is family. He caused them heartache and suffering which he was truly sorry for. He went to AA meetings regularly and completed the 12 Step Program a few times. He owned his short comings and accepted that his family may or may not ever forgive him. He would say, with a hearty laugh, "Well, I may not have been a good example to my boys but I sure was a good "bad" example for them and hopefully they wont follow in my footsteps".

If you're truly sorry for something you've said or done, consider admitting it to those you've harmed. Speak of your sincere sorrow or regret, and ask for forgiveness, without making excuses. Making excuses is justifying your actions, not being sorry for them.

Remember, however, you can't force someone to forgive you. Others need to move to forgiveness in their own time. Whatever happens, commit to treating others with compassion, empathy and respect. Forgiving yourself or someone who has hurt you could be the greatest challenge of your life. But if you choose to forgive, you will join those, like my friend, who are not being destroyed by bitterness, anger, hurt or other toxic emotions. There is nothing quite like living in peace, knowing you are a forgiving person.

Sacred Gratitude

If you want more happiness and joy, gratitude is clearly a crucial quality to cultivate. It is a fullness of heart that moves us from limitation and fear to expansion and love. When we're appreciating something, our ego moves out of the way and we connect with our soul. Gratitude brings our attention into the present, which is the only place where miracles can unfold. The deeper our appreciation, the more we see with the eyes of the soul and the more our life flows in harmony with the creative power of the universe.

The benefits of practicing gratitude are nearly endless. People who take time to reflect upon the things they're thankful for are happier, sleep better, express more compassion and kindness, and even have stronger immune systems.

It can sometimes be difficult to pay much attention to gratitude, particularly when we are ill or there are difficult things happening in our lives and in the world. We may be tempted to think there is nothing to be grateful for. Our tendency is to focus our attention on the negative which is damaging to our minds and our bodies.

Many years ago when I was going through a difficult time a wise friend was trying to help me through it. She said I needed to start a gratitude journal and write in it every day. I just gave her the "look", as I was barely making it from one day to the next. She asked me to name three things I was grateful for and I honestly couldn't think of anything. She then said "You could be grateful that you have toilet paper and light bulbs and gas in your car". It was like a slap in the face that brought me back to reality.

I will never forget her kind wisdom and her teaching me about gratitude that day. She helped me to put things in perspective and be a more grateful person even in the midst of hardship and heartache. It is a lesson that has stayed with me for life.

The idea of a gratitude journal has been around for a long time. Maybe you have tried one and it didn't work or do anything for you. Give it another try. Start by listing 3 things you are grateful for. We can use my friends suggestions.

1. Toilet paper
2. Light bulbs
3. Gas in your car

The University of Southern California did a study that showed when people wrote down more specific reasons why they're grateful for something, they were happier!

Now to be more specific, for each of the initial 3 items, write 5 reasons why you are grateful for each one.

Toilet paper:

1. It's better than newspaper or leaves!
2. Cleanliness
3. Convenience
4. Comfort
5. If you don't have a french Boidae you need the paper!

Light bulbs:

1. Instant light
2. I'm afraid of the dark
3. Having to go back to dripping wax candles, no thanks
4. I know we have light pollution and candles are cool and romantic but I'm a city girl and can't even imagine a pitch black world with no light bulbs
5. I'm thankful I'm not so broke that I can't afford light bulbs, at least in most of my lamps!

Gas in my car:

1. I'm grateful I have enough gas to get to work etc.
2. I may have to budget filling my tank but thankfully I can
3. I live in a city where walking everywhere isn't an option and weather doesn't permit bike transportation year round and the bus system is terrible. I'm very grateful I have a car with gas in the tank!
4. There have been times I was nearly out of gas and couldn't go everywhere I wanted. I'm thankful that isn't one of my problems today.
5. If I end up homeless at least I have my car with gas in it!

The examples may be silly but at the time I was in a deep depression and I had to really reach deep to make myself believe I had anything to be grateful for.

If this exercise is too hard or time consuming to fit into your daily routine, just list one thing in your journal you are grateful for each day, followed by 5 reasons you are grateful for it.

If you commit to a daily gratitude practice and write in your gratitude journal every day it will change your life and attitude. It will teach you to be more positive and not dwell on the negative so much. Cultivating gratitude is a powerful way to fight negativity and anxiety as well as depression.

When you focus on the things that make you feel happy and lucky to be alive, you radiate an infectious optimism that attracts only the best from the world around you.

Being grateful generates good vibrations. Quantum physics applied to positive thinking states that the vibrations of your thoughts affect and modify the reality around you.

Studies have shown that gratitude can lead to increased feelings of social responsibility, and a genuine desire to give back to those less fortunate.

Be Grateful For the People in Your Life

Think about the people you know who are most appreciative of you and let you know it. How do you feel about them? Does their appreciation positively impact your relationship with them? Of course it does! Be grateful for people, their contributions, their talents and their actions and make sure you let them know how you feel.

Humans have a natural hunger for appreciation, the real kind, and being thanked. In a way, being appreciated, and being made aware of it, is one way of letting us know that we matter, and that our efforts at anything and everything we do, actually amount to something. Make it a habit to thank people for their kindness.

Gratitude is an attitude. Gratitude is a choice. And gratitude is a habit. When we consciously practice being grateful for the people, situations and resources around us we begin to attract better relationships and results. The habit will be strengthened as you make the choice each day.

Fill every day with gratitude. As you go through your day, regularly express your gratefulness for everything you can think of, the wonderful day, the beautiful flowers, the sunshine, your spouse, the smile on your child's face, your family's health, and on and on. Let gratitude fill your heart and you'll be surprised to see what a difference this will make. Gratefulness opens the doorway to your Inner Goddess.

Gracious Receiving

She is the essence of innocence and purity, love and divine Knowing. This is why she sustains life and builds empires out of grace, giving, and gratitude; for she is the one that receives.

Most women love to help others and give gifts and compliments but find it very difficult to accept the same in return. If you are uncomfortable being on the receiving end you may want to examine your beliefs on receiving. Ask yourself; Do I feel unworthy? Vulnerable? Embarrassed? Guilty? Loss of control? These are not goddess attributes. A goddess would graciously accept the kindness with gratitude without feeling self-conscious.

Masculine energy is a penetrating force of energy. Feminine energy is the receptive energy that opens. By receiving love, energy, and attention your deep well of feminine energy is filled up.

Receiving Help:

Receiving help is an art-form in itself, and one which I think the world needs more of. Seeking and accepting assistance gives others an opportunity to serve you.

When we are having a difficult time and someone offers to help us, we are usually embarrassed or ashamed or too prideful, and more often than not refuse the help. Maybe we are embarrassed for getting ourselves into the situation that caused our need for help.

To receive is such a beautiful experience if you feel the love and are grateful. If you don't receive well you stop the flow of love. When you receive, you give other people an opportunity to give. Don't let your pride take away their blessings.

When someone helps you and they are struggling too, that's not help, that's love.

Receiving Gifts

When you are given a lovely gift, especially an expensive one, do you feel undeserving of such a grand gesture and don't want to accept it? When someone decides to give you something, it means in their mind, they have already decided that you deserve to be the receiver of the gift. So don't question whether you deserve it or not.

Receiving is not only about you. It's also about the giver. Imagine a well-intention, loving person giving you something and you reject their gifts. How would that make them feel? Unappreciated? Awkward? Embarrassed?

Receiving Compliments

When we are complimented on our beauty we may turn inside out from embarrassment because all we see are our faults and imperfections. You may feel uncomfortable that they have been looking at you. If you are complimented on a job well done, you may belittle your accomplishment and say "It was nothing".

When someone is complimenting you, they are sharing how your actions or behaviors impacted them. They are not asking if you agree. It really takes something for someone to get up the nerve to share the impact you have had on them, and to them, giving you that recognition is liking giving a gift.

Let them share that gift. If their compliment made a difference for you, let them know. It will make their day for them to know they made yours. Become acutely aware of how you respond when people recognize you.

Even if you think the person complementing you has an ulterior motive, just say, "thank you." The more comfortable you become at accepting recognition, the more comfortable you will be with giving it.

Receiving Kindness

When someone gives you love or kindness, accept their kindness and help graciously like the Divine Feminine you are.

When it's your time to receive, it's important for you to embrace the moment. By receiving with tender self-compassion, we're allowing ourselves to be touched by life's gifts.

Conscious Connection to Others

Sometimes it feels new-agey when we hear "we are all connected, we are all one". When we don't even know our neighbors, it is hard to believe we are "one" with strangers across town or on the other side of the world. But the more you learn about the history of the ancients, other cultures and spiritual practices, the more you understand we are all here just passing through this life and headed to the next life. We may look different, dress different and speak different, but we are all in this together!

Before we are born the first vibration we feel is our mother's blood running through her arteries and veins. We vibrate to that primordial rhythm even before we have ears to hear. The first sound we hear is our mother's heartbeat. Before we were conceived, we existed in part as an egg in our mother's ovary. All the eggs a woman will ever carry form in her ovaries while she is a four month old fetus in the womb of her mother. This means our cellular life as an egg began in our grandmother's womb.

Each of us spent five months in our grandmother's womb and she in turn was formed in the womb of her grandmother. We vibrate to the rhythms of our mother's blood before she herself was born. And this pulse is the thread of blood that runs all the way back through the grandmothers to the first mother. We all share the blood of the first mother. We truly are children of one blood.

Our ancient ancestors spent most of their time outdoors. They walked on the earth, worked under the sun, rested under the shade of trees, grew food in the soil, bathed in the oceans and rivers, gazed at the stars and moon at night and worked together as a community for their survival. They lived with the cycles of the moon and the seasons. They slept when it was dark and arose with the sun in the morning. They lived in community and knew they were not alone, that there is life after life, and ways to communicate with the spirit world.

I am in awe and feel very connected to them when I think how we walk on the same earth, live under the same sun, enjoy the rivers and oceans as they did, we gaze at the very same moon and stars they once looked up at, feel the same breezes on our skin, are warmed by the same sun and hear the same ocean waves our ancient ancestors did and as our sisters and brothers do on the other side of the world.

Personal Spirituality

"To me, being spiritual means whispering to trees, laughing with flowers, falling in love with

*sunsets, consulting with the water and worshiping
the stars. One hand to my heart. One hand
to the Earth. And sparkles. Tons of them."*

Spirituality is the freedom and ability to find your own personal path to your purpose and meaning on earth and the here-after. It is about your ability to experience direct personal revelation.

Your Inner Goddess invariably involves how you can best serve others while being true to yourself. You will be surprised how much universal support you garner when you bring a greater spiritual meaning to your physical experience.

Spirituality and Divine Femininity is not an anti-God movement or an anti-religious movement or a radical feminist movement to overthrow and overpower men. It is a recognition that uncontrolled masculine energy has brought us to a point of eminent destruction if we don't turn things around.

We are each unique and individual, we have had different life experiences and formed our own perspectives as a result. We will attract similar souls and united we will be a strong force of change for the betterment of humans, animals, the plant world and Mother Earth.

You only have to read the news to see our world has no moral values or accountability, no matter which subject we choose to think about. Without Divine Feminine intervention there will be no change, only further dishonesty and destruction.

Rise up and be all you can be. Let no man put you down, humiliate you or hold you back or make you think you are weak. Believe me they are more afraid of you than you know. Their day of control and domination of the Divine Feminine is coming to an end. As they lose control they roar louder.

A Goddess Lives in the Present

"You must be completely awake in the present to enjoy the tea. Only in the awareness of the present, can your hands feel the pleasant warmth of the cup. Only in the present, can you savor the aroma, taste the sweetness, appreciate the delicacy. If you are ruminating about the past, or worrying about the future, you will completely miss the experience of enjoying the cup of tea. You will look down at the cup, and the tea will be gone." – Thich Nhat Hanh

It's good to think about the past and future sometimes. Where would you be if we didn't look back over your past successes and mistakes and learn from them? Where would you be if you never planned for the future or prepared yourself for what is to come? In both cases, you likely wouldn't be in a good place.

It's essential to a healthy life to spend some time thinking about the past and the future, the problem comes when focusing too intently or obsessively about it.

One of the aims of mindfulness and a key factor in living a healthy life is to balance your thoughts of the past, the present, and the future. Thinking about any of them too much can have serious negative effects on your life, but keeping the three in balance will help you to be happy and healthy.

It's hard to say what the exact right balance is, but you'll know you've hit it when you worry less, experience less stress on a regular basis, and find yourself living the majority of your life in the present.

Being in the present moment, or the "here and now," means that you are aware and mindful of what is happening at this very moment. You are not distracted by ruminations on the past or worries about the future, but centered in the here and now. All of your attention is focused on the present moment.

When you are aware and present the vast majority of time, you don't need to worry about getting caught up in thoughts of your past or anxiety about your future, you can revisit your past and anticipate what is to come without losing yourself.

Your life is happening right now. This is where it's at. Enjoy your life and the people in it. Make great memories every day so if you are lucky enough to have a tomorrow you can wake up happy and make more great memories. In the end that is all you have anyway.

When my time on earth is up I want to think back on all the happy loving days I was lucky enough to live rather than suffer from regrets, remorse or shame. Don't let pettiness ruin your day.

Modern Goddesses Are Classy

Looking back through ancient history, you will discover that there is a mythical goddess for just about anything. And this is good for us because it makes it easier to find one that we can relate to.

Goddesses have an aura about them that makes them so desirable. They are strong, powerful, wise, beautiful, confident, feminine, gracious and everything else in between.

No matter what lifestyle you follow, if you want to be a classy goddess you have to develop a sense of what is appropriate in every situation. You need to know that people are always watching you, the goddess, and how you act. You have an audience. People notice you.

As divine feminine we are here to bring balance to the world, so how people perceive us is important to further our cause. Perception is reality, and how others perceive you is exactly how people will remember you and either help you or hinder you.

Be Gracious

A divine feminine is always gracious. Treat others the way you want to be treated. Be kind and behave in a positive manner with those around you. If you become over agitated at someone, regardless if they "deserved it" it will always look badly on you because you did not have to react that poorly. However if someone is being inappropriate to you or others, there is no need to be ok with it. Calling someone out for being inappropriate is your goddess right and responsibility. Setting healthy boundaries is also a sign of a goddess who knows her values and worth.

Say Thank You

Having manners and following etiquette begins with saying "thank you". When you don't thank people who put an effort into something that affects you, not only is it rude but you appear to have a sense of entitlement. You must understand that being entitled is one of the worst characteristics to embody.

Be Punctual

Being on time is a common sense rule but some women seem to forget this. When you arrive late to a meeting or an event, you promote a negative perception of your personality and suggest that you do not value the event or the people waiting for you.

Don't forget that people spent their time and energy to create the event or party and a classy goddess would show respect and show up on time.

Look Appropriate for the Occasion

Overdressing, wearing too much makeup or flashy jewelry may look like you are trying way to hard to impress. A divine feminine does not need to prove her worth to anyone, she knows she is worthy already.

You can easily look your best by wearing adequate clothing, just the right amount of accessories and well kept nails (chipped nail polish is not classy!). Less is always more to look elegant and not overdone on any occasion.

By taking responsibility how you look and are perceived by others, will really make you memorable in the best ways possible. When choosing your clothes and accessories, ask yourself, how do I want to be remembered?

Keep Your Word

When it comes to being a classy goddess, keeping your word is essential. If you can't keep a promise it is better not to promise at all. You loose all respect from others when you go back on your word and don't following through.

Put Your Cell Phone Away

Be attentive to those around you. Keeping your cell phone in hand has become an addiction but is also very offensive to those around you. When you are constantly looking at your phone, texting, playing games or talking on your phone, you send a disappointing message to the person or people you are with that they are unimportant and you don't care that much about them.

Don't Be Rude

If you have to go out in public, chances are you are going to run into someone who is rude or just down right mean. But that doesn't mean you have to stoop to their level, and confronting them on their level never turns out well.

Being a divine feminine means being kind to everyone. But there are times when they aren't returning the favor. You can't take it personally. Don't be entitled, easily offended or feel disrespected. If you let your emotions take hold of you and react crudely, that is the image others will have of you. Remember how you are perceived by people is how "you are" in their eyes.

Dealing with rude people is just a fact of life because someone is always unhappy about something. You can't control other people but you can control yourself. So when people are being rude, just be courteous, no matter what. You are strong enough to take it and you just may be that someone they might need.

The more often you handle situations with poise and a gentle demeanor the easier it becomes to keep doing it.

Don't Be Selfish

Being egotistical will get you nowhere. Some people are more selfish than others, it has always been so. You know you are selfish when you always wonder things like; "What's in it for me?" or "How can I benefit from this situation?" or "How can I manipulate this person to get what I want?". When you are selfish and choose not to change, is when rudeness sets in and you are oblivious to the fact that you are hurting people. Being selfish is not divine.

Be Informed

Goddesses possess infinite wisdom. This is why it is so important to constantly invest in yourself and be informed and aware of what is going on around you and in the world. It's so easy to get lost in the entertainment and amusement world but you must remember to put edification over entertainment.

You don't need bigger boobs, you need to read better books. It is much better for your mind and soul.

CHAPTER 6

Let it Go!

Accept what is, let go of what was,
and have faith in what will be.

Sometimes it's better to just let things be, let people go, don't fight for closure, don't ask for explanations, don't chase answers and don't expect people to understand where you are coming from. Learn to be okay with people not knowing your side of the story, you have nothing to prove to anyone. "Let it Go" is about taking care of yourself first and letting others take responsibility for their actions without trying to save or punish them.

Let Go of Being the Nice Girl

"Never underestimate the power of a
kind woman. Kindness is a choice that
comes from incredible strength".

Merriam Webster defines Kind as "wanting and liking to do good things and to bring happiness to others." In short, kind is something we own instead of something we fulfill. Kind is something we can decide about ourselves, a gift that we can decide to bestow.

A Divine Feminine is kind not "nice". In many cross-cultural myths, we hear of references to the ancient Goddesses as being kind, though, just as often, Goddesses chose to be deeply wild, sharp and severe. But we never hear of a Goddess being "nice". Nice isn't big enough for the vastness of a Goddess.

When we devote ourselves to being nice girls we give up both agency and power. At its root, the very world "nice" is something that is defined by others. Nice is a title that is bestowed upon you by those you have pleased, a reward for agreeability.

Nice is something we must mold ourselves to be. Your skill at fulfilling this role is wholly judged, decided and anointed by others. As nice girls, we don't have the power to decide whether or not we are good; this lies directly in the hands of those who judge us to be nice. Nice is mild and forgettable.

Kind Divine Feminine women take into account what is best for everyone, which means standing up to those that cause hurt and wrong- doing and recognize that calling people out, is just as important for the healing of the offender as the offended. Nice girls are quiet when injustices happen, especially to their own selves. How many times have you reacted to injustice by being nice, quiet, agreeable or mild, when you should have been "kind"?

It is kindness, not niceness, that truly makes difference in the world. How different would this world be if we had been raised to be kind women?

The Divine Feminine, has been starved from our earth. Kindness, and truly bold-hearted compassion, is what will reawaken balance once more. Look in the mirror and ask yourself "What would a goddess do?"

The world needs more kind women and fewer women who are still little girls. It is time to question your taught beliefs about being "nice" and agreeable. It's no wonder we doubt ourselves when we haven't been taught to stand up for ourselves and others in distress. Burn your old role of being "a nice girl".

Statements for Divine Feminine to practice:

- You interrupted me. I'm not finished talking.
- No.
- That isn't funny.
- That isn't appropriate.
- That won't be necessary.
- Leave me alone.
- You're making me uncomfortable.
- Stop ignoring what I'm saying.

Unleash your Inner Goddess and remember, standing up to those that cause hurt and wrong- doing and recognize that calling people out, is just as important for their healing as it is for the offended.

Let Go of Fear

"Fear is the thief of dreams."~Gandhi

A Goddess is not fearful and never concerns herself with trivial things. She has been around for a long time and knows the ways of the Universe. She is your soul, she is you.

Too many people live fear-based lives. Fear gets in the way of your happiness, it causes unnecessary anxiety and suffering. It limits your opportunities and possibilities.

Everyone is afraid of something. However, it's how you approach that fear that really matters. If you hide from your fear then you may be holding yourself back. This can then lead to regret later.

Most women fear not being enough or what other people are

going to think of them. In an interview Stevie Nicks said in the beginning of her career with Fleetwood Mac she was surrounded by men in the industry, there were very few female rock singers at the time, and she could have easily been intimidated. Rather than being fearful she walked into a new room like a Goddess and was treated with the respect she commanded and never had a problem. She said the secret was "You just walk into the room fearless, never let them think for a minute that you couldn't totally take them down."

Fear Based Decisions:

We make fear-based decisions out of insecurity or out of a feeling of scarcity, or fear of being judged or rejected.

We fear change and the unknown. You're afraid of things changing because if they change, you don't know what they'll change to. Let your fear of the unknown be replaced with curiosity.

Don't cling on to anything too tightly because everything must and will change. To exist is to change. To change is to mature. To mature is to go on creating oneself endlessly.

The greatest prison people live in is the fear of what other people think. You shouldn't care or be afraid of what people think. Why should the opinions of others matter to you? All that should matter is what is right for you. Everyone is different. They get to make their choices for their life and so do you. If they stick their nose in your business don't let it be your problem.

You are a magnificent Divine Being more powerful than you ever imagined. If you remembered who you really are, you would never be afraid. If you knew who was with you at all times, you would not be afraid.

The phrase "Do not be afraid" is written in the bible 365 times. That's a daily reminder to live life fearlessly. Once you become fearless your life becomes limitless.

A goddess isn't wimpy and fearful. Be kind and strong. You are a fearless goddess.

Any decision you make that is based on fear, is driven by the wrong motives and is less likely to give you the desired outcome. A fear-based decision turns into regret.

Many times we are afraid to make a decision for fear it will be the wrong choice. Most of the time there is not a right or wrong choice, just a different choice which will take us down a path with different life lessons to learn, people to meet and things to do. If it turns out it was a bumpy road you will come out stronger and smarter for it. Be adventurous don't be stifled.

Do the best you can to make the best choices for yourself. Live your life on your terms, using your own beliefs. Fear of making the wrong choice stems from our taught belief of good and evil, right and wrong. Let it go. If a belief creates fear in you, that belief is not in alignment with your true self.

When we let fear rule our decision-making, we relinquish control over our lives, one decision at a time. Little by little, we become more reactive and less proactive. We don't participate in the direction of the path we take, we just take it, without asking questions.

Growth Based Decisions:

Growth-based decisions focus on growth, progress, and improvement. You should always keep these three ideas in sharp focus when it comes to decision-making and you should know that although they're not the complete solution, they're definitely a big part of that puzzle.

With growth-based decisions you feel it in your body: an expansion of your chest, ideas in your mind, a feeling of competence increasing. A feeling of freedom expanding. That means owning your choices and confidently making decisions based on strategy, love, and growth. A growth-based decision becomes the story of your life later.

Whether you are wanting to earn a degree, or leave a job you hate, or travel the world, and so on, you need to overcome the fears associated with these goals in order to have a happy fulfilled life.

Let Go of Perfection

"There is no need to be perfect to inspire others. Let people get inspired by how you deal with your imperfections."

Most of us have been brought up to strive to be perfect in all we do. Obviously the problem with that is that perfection isn't possible and we will always fall short. Instead of positive reinforcement as a child that we are loved and good enough as we are, we grow up with a nagging belief that we aren't "good enough" no matter how hard we try.

Like many of you I also I grew up in a religion that put an emphasis on perfection and always doing the right thing, being nice and obedient. When facing decisions I wasn't confident in myself which molded me into a people pleaser, always putting others happiness and needs before my own and feeling like I wasn't ever "good enough" or worthy enough.

Never at home or in church was I taught to believe in myself, to love myself, to put my happiness first, or that I was important or powerful. Looking back on it I was molded into a sweet girl who's purpose was to bring comfort and happiness to others and my happiness should come from their gratitude, love and approval.

Some of the biggest regrets in my life have been decisions I have made trying to do the "right thing". I didn't know enough to question "the right thing for who and according to who?". I thought it was selfish to choose the "right thing for me" instead of someone else.

I didn't have enough self confidence to think for myself or question the beliefs I had been taught, I just took them as "true" and tried my best to live a "worthy" life. Living a worthy life meant you have to earn everything and be deserving of it. This is a paralyzing belief system, as being perfect and being worthy enough is never obtainable.

My favorite people and best friends were always the rebels, the ones who dared to speak up and buck the system and break the rules. I wished so much I had the courage to be like them, it looked so fun and daring. In school I was the most timid and shy of them all but the wild girls loved me and took me in because I was in awe of them, which encouraged them to be more outrageous and shock me just to see my reactions.

At the time I just thought I was shy, that it was a personality trait. I didn't realize that I had been so brainwashed, controlled and micro managed by family and church that I had no identity of my own and was out of touch with the real world.

This naivete really slowed my progress to become the person I am today. I know there are so many women out there who are in the same place I use to be. I want to help you to get out of that brainwashed mind set and let go of the old beliefs that are holding you back from your divine happiness.

You are a worthy and deserving soul just because you are here and where you came from. Your Inner Goddess has already done all the work required of her to come to earth to have a human experience, and you are She.

The world isn't perfect, people aren't perfect, and we are perfectly imperfect just the way we are. We are wise knowledgeable souls on earth at this time for a purpose. Perfection is not our goal nor is it the most important thing in our earthy experiences. We were born to make mistakes so we can learn and grow. If we were perfect or meant to be perfect we would have stayed in the unseen world.

Let Go of Expectations

"Expectation is the root of all
heartache" William Shakespeare

An expectation about the behavior or performance of another person, may or may not be realistic, which may give rise to the emotion of disappointment, over and over again. Let go of trying to control others and having strong opinions of how you think they should be.

My mother has an expression she has used for as long as I can remember "We all get to be who we are".

We gladly embrace this freedom for ourselves, but all too often rather than allowing others "to be who they are", we place expectations on them, such as how we think they should be or what they should do and how they should do it, and are then disappointed when they don't live up to our expectations.

Or we are in a relationship with someone and believe they will "change" because they love us so much, or our love blinds us to their lack of self motivation and we choose to believe they aren't living up to their potential because all they need is the "right" opportunity or the "right" person to love them. If this is you, You are in la la land.

If your boyfriend is a mama's boy, he will always be a mama's boy. He will not grow out of it or change just because you are in the picture. If you don't want to deal with that, don't waste time waiting for him to change, just bow out and move on.

Here's the Deal:

Number One: If you aren't happy with someone as they are, you shouldn't be in a relationship with them.

You are not honoring that they get to be who they are. You want them to change and be the way you want them to be.

Number Two: You can't change or save another person. If they ever do change it will be because they want to and they are ready to. You have nothing to do with it. Believing someone will learn their lesson, mature or grow up is a waste of time, because some people never do and they are good with that. If you want someone to change or be different you are not with the right person.

You get to be who you are and so do they. You wouldn't appreciate someone trying to change or mold you into someone different so they would love or respect you more than the way you already are.

Many divorced women with children are continually exasperated with their ex-husbands because;

- they don't follow through and do what they say they will do
- they forget it is their weekend with the kids
- they change the agreed upon plans
- they are late or don't pay the child support etc.

They get upset and act surprised every time. Their expectations of the ex-husband are unrealistic because if he actually followed through and was a role model dad and ex-husband she probably never would have divorced him to begin with. Consider that maybe he is doing the best he can, with what he has to work with and who he really is.

You really have no business placing expectations on others in the first place. And when you stop it you will find peace in allowing others to be who they are, even if you don't like it. At the same time you will be more joyful being who you truly are without worrying about what others think or expect of you.

It isn't other people who cause you suffering, but your own thoughts and expectations about them and who they "should" be. Expecting someone to be who You want them to be is self imposed misery.

Don't blame people for disappointing you. Blame yourself for expecting too much from them and not accepting them as they are. Expect nothing. Appreciate everything.

Let Go of Resistance

Letting go of expectations requires you to stop resisting and practice acceptance. This applies to yourself as well as others.

It is not always easy to like people who behave in unkind or problematic ways. You can, however, still extend compassion by recognizing that everyone has their own circumstances to deal with. Accepting someone doesn't mean you have to spend time with them.

When we practice acceptance of ourselves, we confront the source of our regrets, fears, and insecurity and come to peace with them. By doing this, we take away their power to affect our lives and have the ability to choose to let go of the event, heal, and move on with our lives. This allows us to become truly free and no longer held back by the event.

To learn acceptance, try taking the emotion out of an event and see it for what it was. When you accept something, you are no longer attached or clouded by the emotion. Acceptance is being able to experience an event, memory, or action without emotion and without expectation. When you truly accept something for what it is, you are not tied to changing the outcome nor do you wish the event never happened. You let go of all resistance. You let go of all expectation. You simply let it be.

Sometimes we resist getting off a path we know is not right for us and the universe steps in and knocks us off the path to point us in a different direction. Example; If a girl steals your man, your best revenge is to let her keep him. It may not have been what you wanted but deep down you know, or you will come to accept, that was not your life to live, not your path or the highest purpose for your life. Let go of the pain and let go of the resistance to let him go. Letting go of resistance will set you free.

When you are able to accept your past, for whatever it was, you will be free to move on with your life and become the beautiful Divine Feminine woman you are meant to be, without bitterness or a hardened heart.

Let Go Of Judgement

"Once you awake you will have no interest in judging those who sleep." James Blanchard

We have all judged and been judged. It might be over small things, or over bigger issues. Regardless, we do it.

Judging others has more to do with you than it does others. This is because often our judgement on others show our own weaknesses, soft-spots, and insecurities. Most judgments we make about people are based on lack of information. We make assumptions and judgments based on what we see, not on facts.

Most times, you are judging people you see out in public, at a restaurant, grocery store, shopping mall, drivers on the road, etc., people you know nothing about. You have no insight into why they dress, act, or talk the way they do. All you know is that you see something about them that you consider being 'wrong', 'different' or 'inappropriate'.

People have differences in the ways of seeking happiness and fulfillment, which make it hard for others to accept some behaviors. As humans we tend to judge others by our personal standards and beliefs. When we aren't mindful about compassion and tolerance we have a tendency to criticize those who are different or do things differently than we do.

When you judge you hurt other people. It can perpetuate stereotypes. Whether they are based on gender, race, ethnicity, spirituality, appearance or some other attribute, they'll always be bad news. Stereotypes force people, you included, to feel as if they have to meet certain standards instead of living a free life full of happiness. You increase negativity in your heart and in what you put out into the world.

Whenever you pass judgement on another person, you are probably also judging yourself pretty harshly. It is not an easy thing to do, but you have to stop judging yourself and focus more on the positive aspects of yourself. This will make it easier to see good in others as well. There is no reason to be hard on yourself.

People sometimes judge others because they forget that all human beings make mistakes. Remember how it feels to be judged. It doesn't feel good to judge or be judged. Try to remember this the next time you are judging or criticizing. Try to open the door of your heart to expand your awareness and self-acceptance.

A Goddess doesn't judge. She is self confident enough to not be worried about what others think of her and she is too busy living her life to care about what others are doing or how they do it. She may be curious and she may be amused but she doesn't bother herself to judge.

Let Go of Negativity

In my opinion, this is one of the first steps to becoming a better you. Negativity can hold you back from many things in life, especially happiness. When you are carrying around a victim attitude of "I have the worst luck" or "nothing goes right in my life" then that is what you will get in return. Your mind creates your reality. Not because of some magical universe phenomenon, but because of your choosing to only look at the negative things in your life, and not giving any attention to all the positives.

*"If one good thing happens today and a
hundred bad things, talk about that good
thing a thousand times. You've just got to get
happy, that's all it takes." Abraham Hicks*

If you can get into the habit of automatically thinking positively you will be able to cut 90% of the stress signals which make your body believe you are not safe, which can actually make you ill.

Thoughts are habits and the more we think a certain way we reinforce those thinking habits. When you are a habitually positive thinker the stresses in your life don't affect you as much and therefore you are less likely to be fearful, angry or give power to negative beliefs.

Let Go of Old Stories

To move forward in your life you need to examine the traumas and old stories you hold inside of your being that need to be cleared. Stories that you are not enough, you are unworthy, undeserving, and ways of being that are no longer reflective of who you are. These stories may have served you in the past, or not, but they wont serve you as you unfold and expand. Be OK with allowing "what was" to fall away, like old skin.

Patriarchy

According to Taoism, the feminine yin and the masculine yang forces are two opposite parts of a whole reality. None of them are good or bad; what is good is a balance between the two; what is bad is yin yang imbalance; however, both are necessary in order to create harmony in any change. We therefore need male as well as female, men and women, to live and reproduce. Every person is both an individual and integrated in relations, being antonymous and part of society.

Regrettably the modern world view perceives man as being more important than, and prioritized over women; human over nature; male over female; master over slave; white over colored; rich over poor; adult over child; individual over social; modern over traditional; civilized over primitive; developed over undeveloped; culture over nature; theory over practice; mechanical over ecological; science over experience; rationality over intuition; reason over emotion; quantity over quality.

In Modern Patriarchy, the feminine yin is marginalized and therefore prevented from functioning as the necessary balancing factor, so the masculine yang force rules unrestricted. Modern society is founded on an antiquated perception of reality that is both limited and limiting.

What is patriarchy?

"Patriarchy" (derived from patriarch in Greek) is a term for societies in which male is the favored gender, and in which men hold power, dominion and privilege. Male power in a patriarchy can be found in family, community, religious and governmental structures.

For the last 5,000 years the global rule of men, or patriarchy, has wreaked havoc and destructive chaos on earth and all her children. This grievous fact is hardly noticed by anyone other than those who are victimized by it, mostly women and children. And even then, those who suffer at the hands of male rule are often blamed for that which is inflicted upon them.

Because patriarchy defines men as the rulers, men's and women's roles are strictly defined and, in a sense, enforced. Women must be seen as inferior, weaker, generally less capable, less intelligent, and less worthy. The same pressure exists for men to conform to particular roles. One example is that men must be tough and strong, must not cry, must not back down, must be willing to get into physical altercations to solve problems.

Because patriarchy demands that those in power conform to a specific set of rules, ones that require the suppression of feelings and include a lack of empathy, patriarchy is the root of many of the world's problems, i.e., war, colonization, rape, sexism, racism, destruction of the environment, "domestic" violence, terrorism, pornography, sexual slavery, to name a few.

Before patriarchy took over our ancient hunter-gathering ancestors lived as just one of the species in a community of species. They did not see themselves in any way special or above other species. They knew and understood that they were a part of an interconnected web of life. They did not see themselves as owning the land but as being a part of the land. Although they hunted and gathered, this was done with respect for the other species they shared the land with, and with gratitude. All other species were honored whether plant or animal. Even the stones, and hills, and rivers and streams and the land itself was honored as being the body of Mother Earth. Everything was sacred, everything was spirit.

Once patriarchy took over and ruled they went from seeing themselves being part of the land to owning the land and deciding who lives on it and who dies. And doing with the land as they wished; you goats can live on this land and because you do, we own you and can do with you as we wish. But all you other species who compete with the goats or who eat them, you now die. Wheat, you can grow on this land, but all other plants, we now kill you. For we own this land. This thinking is entitlement without accountability.

The early church justified this behavior and entitlement by using their new God, their one true God, who rather than being a god of nature now says "Let us make mankind....rule over the fish in the sea and the birds in the sky, over the livestock and all the wild animals, and over the creatures that move along the ground." (Genesis 1:26)

In hunter-gathering times other species may have been in competition with humans for resources. However, at no time did our hunter-gathering ancestors set out to systematically wipe out all the wolves or lions or bears where they lived. Other species were treated with great respect and reverence, and often refereed to as brothers and sisters. The idea of deliberately waging totalitarian war against another species would have been inconceivable. It would have been crossing the line, and not in accordance with Great Spirit. It would have been an abomination.

It is time for all women and men to rise and unite our voices, hearts, and minds to change and transform that which does not serve life. The archaic patriarchal reign in human history must come to an end.

We shouldn't discount all men and their ability to be upstanding divine individuals, we just have to keep high standards and accountability in check.

How to Combat Patriarchy

- Support a spectrum of ideas of what a "real man" looks like, such as those that are compassionate and responsible. We need to stop holding up "macho" or the "tough, silent type" as the gold standard for maleness.

- Push for a culture of excellence to hold men/boys accountable for their language and actions. This means countering the "boys will be boys" idea. Patriarchy thrives because we live in a culture of male entitlement. Society behaves as if men are entitled to treat women in a chauvinistic dehumanizing manner. By maintaining a "boys will be boys" mentality, we teach women to tolerate male aggression or change their behavior to avoid it. This is not the right approach.

- From an early age, many try to encourage boys to "hide their emotions." So whether you work with kids, have a child, or want to contribute to reducing sexual violence, we need to train males how to express themselves. Teach boys and men how to authentically communicate their emotions and listen empathetically to others. We shouldn't associate emotions with weakness.

- Stop telling young girls that they are bossy just because they want to be class president. Encourage girls to take charge. These girls are our future leaders. Don't forget, "little girls with big dreams become women with a vision".

- Defy unrealistic beauty standards set up just for the pleasure of men to look at. Trying to live up to media images of attractive bodies, makeup, hair, and fashion steals countless hours from women's lives. Love yourself more, fight the power of the media by trying one of those messy, undone, "I woke up like this" looks and occasionally share your just-okay-looking face with the world! This is not because you don't care what you look like, it's because you can be comfortable being your authentic self.

- Female sexuality is routinely exploited in the mass media. Scantily clad women in advertising and full nudity in movies and television are commonplace and yet, many women are shamed for breast-feeding in public. These conflicting views on female sexuality create a confusing landscape of expectations that women must navigate on a daily basis.

- Gender roles are when society comes up with a set of things each gender should do. For example, the female is considered more of a nurturer than the male, or the male is the main 'bread winner.' Basically, fixed ideas of what is masculine, and what is feminine. These ideas are harmful to both men and women. Because men also can be nurturing, and women can be the main bread winner. Why does it matter who feeds the baby or who brings home the most money? Why can't both genders be nurturing and bring home the bacon?

- Patriarchy dictates that girls should hate other girls. It says that we should be in constant competition with each other and that we have to be the most beautiful "one" at all times. Because after all, the prettiest girl gets the boy. This may have been true in the 1800s, but in the 2000's we should stop seeing each other as rivals, and more as sisters instead. Women standing together is patriarchy's biggest threat.

Without fear, you need to let go of the old stories you don't resinate with, that are not in alignment with your soul or don't bring you joy. Change your story, change your beliefs and change the way you live your life.

Let Go Of Thinking Feminism Is A Bad Thing

What is feminism?

The term first appeared during the 1870s in France as féminisme although there has been some speculation that it may have been used before then. At the time, the word referred to women's freedom or emancipation.

Almost all modern societal structures are patriarchal and are constructed in such a way that men are the dominant force in making the majority of political, economic, and cultural decisions. Feminism focuses on the idea that since women comprise one-half of the world population, true social progress can never be achieved without the complete and spontaneous participation of women.

Feminism by its definition stands for equal social, political and economic opportunities for women, who have been systematically oppressed for millennia.

Feminism is a campaign for equal pay and opportunity in the workplace, paid maternity leave, (to name a few issues). Additionally, feminists campaign against domestic violence, discrimination, sexual harassment, and rape. It refers to any actions, especially organized, that promote changes in society to end patterns that have disadvantaged women.

Unequal salaries are still pervasive in the workforce. Despite the Equal Pay Act of 1963, on average, a woman still earns only 80.5 cents for every dollar a man earns. According to data from the U.S. Census Bureau, women's median annual earnings in 2017 were $14,910 less than that of their male counterparts.

The goal of feminism is to create non-discrimination, which is essential for creating equality to ensure that no one is denied their rights due to factors such as race, gender, language, religion, sexual orientation, gender identity, political or other beliefs, nationality, social origin, class, or wealth status.

What woman would be against that? Why would you be against yourself?

Criticisms Of Feminism

Criticism of feminism is sometimes referred to as anti-feminism. Historically, criticism of feminism has been grounded in standing in opposition of the demands of the feminist movement. For example, many people were against women's right to vote during the suffrage movement. Other opponents disagree with access to birth control and reproductive rights, women's involvement in the labor force, and women's attainment of higher education. Most of these stances are rooted in the idea that feminism is contrary to traditional and religious beliefs.

Opponents suggest that feminism is the demoralization of society. Other critics of feminism contend that feminism promotes a dislike of men, boys, and the male gender. They suggest that feminism brings women's issues to a higher level of importance and disregards the needs of men. This attitude, they believe, is harmful to both men and women. None of which is true, but propaganda to remain in control.

Feminism was originally a positive movement, focused on giving women the basic rights God intends for every human being to have. Tragically, radical feminism now focuses on destroying all distinctions in the roles of men and women, making any reference to gender or gender identity unacceptable. As with all things, "extreme" and "radical" is usually not a good thing. Feminism is an umbrella term which has taken on many causes with varying approaches.

Feminism VS Femininity

Contrary to the anti-feminism propaganda, you can be feminine and a feminist. You can be religious and a feminist. You can be a wife and mom and be a feminist. Believing in equal rights and opportunities doesn't automatically make you masculine, anti-religion or a man hater.

Feminine: The state of being feminine, womanly or ladylike in behavior and appearance. Femininity is a quality or set of attributes affiliated with women.

Feminism: A social theory or political movement arguing that legal and social restrictions on females must be removed in order to bring about equality of both sexes. Feminism is a movement.

Being a feminine woman entails so many things. However, social influence and the history of men mistreating women have given femininity a wrong connotation which is weakness. This is probably why neo-feminists do not subscribe to femininity.

But if you think about it, when a feminine woman asserts herself fully while fighting for her rights, this makes her fight even more reasonable and honorable. Femininity in females is the result of nature and nurture.

Femininity Compliments Feminism

Feminism should be about fighting to be treated fairly as a human while embracing and maintaining your original self. By being womanly, you are making a statement saying, "I am proudly a woman and I deserve to be treated right. I do not have to be a man. I am enough as a female human being."

There is no point in declaring sexual or gender ambiguity to get what you want. You can be a woman with a compassionate heart, a fierce soul, a hot body, and a sharp brain! Don't be afraid to strut in your high heels and still demand your right as a human being.

Being feminist is a belief that women should be able to make choices best for themselves and have the same equal opportunities as men to make their choices. Feminism is about women being free to choose how to dress, behave, etc. You can be a feminist and be very feminine or not at all feminine or feminine in some ways and not in others. What is considered feminine varies from culture to culture and personal views. The most important thing is that the woman makes the choice.

Ladies, what's important is to, love yourself, all of you, and show up like that, always. That's true feminism. Nobody says you can't wear makeup and still be a boss.

CHAPTER 7

Divine Feminine Relationships

"When you stop expecting people to be perfect, you can like them for who they are." Donald Miller

Relationship With Yourself

'The greatest thing in the world is to know how to belong to oneself.' The French philosopher Michel de Montaigne

You Belong To Yourself Before You Belong To Anyone Else

A Divine Feminine is not looking for a knight in shining armor. She does not rely on a man for a complete life, happiness or self worth. Her life is hers and where a man is a great complement, it is not an essential element.

You belong to yourself before you belong to anyone else. When you know who you are and who you descend from, it is much easier to be free of fear, have self-love, self-care and self-respect.

We came to this earth as powerful, knowledgeable souls with a purpose, with a mission. While on our journey we will have many rolls and relationships, changing with the seasons of our life. When our journey comes to an end we will return home with our stories and life lessons we could have only experienced with a physical body.

We came to earth at this time as Divine Feminine women to bring balance to the world and restore ancient wisdom that has been lost and forgotten. For the last few thousand years women's statice has been reduced to being subservient and obedient. Women have not been taught to believe in themselves or that they possess any divinity.

You are a powerful, sacred spiritual being. You are not anyone's earthly possession. No one owns you. You are not a toy for anyone's amusement.

We are here to right this wrong perception, this old story, this brainwashing, that women are too weak and too emotional to be independent and self reliant, therefore need to be dominated and controlled.

For the most part, women have not been told how special and powerful they really are. We have been trained to believe we have to look outside of ourselves for assistance and answers. We look to our parents, teachers, friends, husbands, clergy, government, health professionals, anyone who we think is more knowledgeable, capable, or powerful than we are. We pray to God to help us before believing we might be able to turn within ourselves and find our own way, our own answers.

Everything you need and want to know is already inside you. You are a wise soul with all the wisdom you needed to come to earth. You are wise, strong and independent or you wouldn't be here. You have the ability to develop your intuition, meditate and journey to the spirit world for guidance. We have many sacred ancestors willing to help us, if we just ask. In our DNA is the rich history of the wise, strong and powerful divine feminine ancestors.

Don't wait for someone else to appreciate you, love you,

acknowledge you or save you. You are a Divine Goddess. Stand strong in knowing who you are and who you belong to. You belong to yourself before you belong to anyone else. When you choose to share yourself and part of your life with someone, it is their honor not their right.

Self-Love

Even as an adult, the concept of loving myself eluded me. Like many on a spiritual path, I became very good at compassion for others, but had no idea what self-love meant. Little by little, I've learned that it starts with self-esteem, self-acceptance, and finally self-compassion and self-love, all progressive stages.

Whereas self-esteem is an evaluation and acceptance is an attitude, love combines both feeling and action. Contrary to what many believe, self-love is healthy. It's neither selfish, nor self-indulgent, and neither egotism, nor narcissism. Actually, egotists and narcissists don't love themselves at all. A "big ego" is compensation for lack of self-love.

Most people think too little of themselves, not too much, and often falling in love is merely a compensation for inner emptiness, loneliness, and shame. No wonder most relationships fail (including those who stay together).

You are the center of your universe. It all starts and ends with you. You're going to be with yourself for eternity. Which means you want to operate from a place of self-love, rather than self-loathing.

Western society has been influenced by the Christian belief that we're basically sinful, and thus self-love was considered sinful. But since the Bible says, "Love thy neighbor as thyself," how can loving your neighbor be a virtue and self-love be a vice? You're part of humanity as worthy of love as the next person. Many kind or religious people are able to love others, but unable to love themselves.

They believe having a high regard for themselves is indulgent, conceited, arrogant, or selfish. The opposite is true. The greater your love of self, the greater will be your love for others. The opposite is also true; hatred of others is indicative of self-hatred.

Did you need to love yourself as an innocent infant? Of course not, we came into this world as free spirits, untouched by the conditioning of society and inundated in our wonder for life. You were born Divine. One of the biggest lies told to you was that you were born in sin.

Faith is the foundation for self-love, no matter what religion or system you believe in. Believing in something opens up your soul to the beauty of belief and trust itself. When you explore your spirituality, it will take you on a journey of learning things about yourself. And those new thoughts, feelings, passions, and raw emotions will make you appreciate yourself for being authentically you. This will enhance your intuition and help to make decisions based on your gut.

The highest form of love is acceptance. Accept your humanness, flaunt your flaws; otherwise, what you resist will persist. We do not transcend what we deny and resist, we transcend what we can graciously accept. When we surrender to our imperfection, something magical happens: that love and acceptance turns into poetry.

Love is a Divine Feminine quality. The act of self-care is a feminine quality. Loving and nurturing yourself is a feminine quality all goddesses need to develop more.

- Self-love is the act of learning how to love yourself and accept yourself unconditionally and without any reservation about how incredibly 'YOU' you are.
- Self-love is a basic necessity, a fundamental positive value that leads to inner peace and happiness.

- Self-love is the action we take to ensure we are being and accepting our authentic selves by tending to our needs. We must prioritize self-love in order to complete any self-care activities that nurture our well-being and tend to our needs.
- Self-love is honoring your intuition and trusting that it will guide you in the right direction.
- Self-love is honoring your heavenly mother and father, your friends and ancestors who love you and are cheering you on and wishing you love and joy as a human being.

We will never accept ourselves if we approach life with the fear-based mind set of right and wrong. Instead of right and wrong, consider what's helpful and harmful. You never know, the very things about you that you presume wrong, might be exactly what the world needs!

The love you seek exists within you. Love from other people can only make you happy if it expands the love you already have within. And loving others can only originate from self-love: a reflection or expansion of the love you have for yourself. Once you learn to love and accept yourself as you are, the good, the bad, and the ugly, it is easy to accept others without judgement and expectations and love them as they are.

Nourish yourself daily with healthy activities; good nutrition, exercise, proper sleep, intimacy, and healthy social interactions, with lots of time for fun, adventure, and relaxation. When you fuel and take care of your body properly, you'll have optimum energy and vitality which builds upon self-esteem. Self-esteem and self-love go hand in hand, and participating in things you're good at will boost endorphins and bring out the best version of yourself.

Another important benefit of self-love is better mental health. People who love themselves are less likely to suffer from anxiety or depression; self-love also paves the way to a positive mind set which is an essential ingredient for success in life and for mental well-being.

Relationship With Your Body

"If tomorrow women woke up and decided they really liked their bodies, just think of how many industries would go out of business." Gail Dines

Love Your Goddess Body

We women can often feel insecure, whether it's because of our size, shape, height, etc. We find a billion things that are not perfect with us and we frequently compare ourselves to other women. But do you think that Aphrodite ever compared herself to Athena or vice versa? No! They each embraced their divine power and owned their beauty.

A Divine Feminine knows her beauty is more than skin deep. She realizes that true beauty is about being comfortable with who she is. The Divine Feminine is the life-giving force. It is not something to take for granted. It is magical, mystical and very special. Your life is special. Take time to honor the life and body that you have been given.

The earthly bodies we get are subject to our parents and ancestors genes and DNA. Throughout history the ideas of beauty change from stick thin to curvy and voluptuous, flat butt to big butt, short hair to long hair, fair skin to dark skin etc.

The important thing is you have a physical body! Loving yourself is accepting the body you were given is enough. Loving your body doesn't happen overnight. If you've been hating your body for years, it's going to take a little time to repair that relationship. But it's possible and worth it because when you love your body, you take better care of it and healthy eating and exercise stops feeling like a punishment and starts to come naturally.

Does it feel weird to say "I love my body"? Try accepting your body first. Start with "My body is ok as it is". You don't need to find yourself sexy or attractive or love your body from the get-go. That's not nearly as important as being ok with your body. Body acceptance can help bridge the gap between body hate and body love.

Do you realize how much your body loves you? It is always trying to keep you alive. It makes sure you breathe while you sleep, stopping cuts from bleeding, fixing broken bones, finding ways to beat the illness that might get you. Your body literally loves you so much, it's time to start loving it back. We forget how magical it is to just wake up in the morning and get one more day.

There is a long waiting list of souls waiting to come to earth. We are lucky to be here now in this transformational time. To be overly obsessed with how your body looks is very petty in the big picture of things.

If you find yourself hating your body, for whatever reason, it isn't really your body that is the problem. It is your lack of self-love and self-acceptance and liking yourself. You are blaming your body for your problems, and to be honest you probably worry about what other people are thinking and saying about you. Walk away from judgmental people.

Certainly pay attention to how you look. Take pleasure in wearing good clothes and being clean and well groomed. It makes you feel good. People will also look at you differently. Remember that every human being wants to be found in the company of smart, intelligent, successful people. You can soon be a center of attraction if you radiate a positive, sharp look with self-confidence. It can very easily make the difference between success and failure in all walks of life.

The important thing to remember here is that everyone's opinion of you matters much less than what you think about yourself. After all, you are with yourself each and every moment of your existence, and know yourself better than anyone could ever claim to. Love yourself. Take care of yourself. What would a goddess do?

Relationships With Other Women

Find Your Tribe

Women have always banded together, even when they found themselves in male dominated societies. Old fashioned sewing circles and quilting bees, Saturday afternoon teas and Sunday lunches, volunteer groups, community services, neighborhood communities, social clubs, PTA, bridge clubs and charity organizations, gave women time to meet and work with one another, to communicate, cooperate and widen their circle of friends.

Women touch, embrace, laugh and cry together. They share food, feelings, thoughts, and ideas. They support and encourage each other. They lend things, give gifts, and do favors. Some find in women's groups the closest relationships of their lives.

You may need to find a new "tribe" of like-minded individuals to continue on your new spiritual journey, health journey, or other lifestyle or career changes you wish to make.

Once you decide to let go of old beliefs that no longer serve you or bring you joy, you usually are confronted with resistance from friends and family who don't want to change their ways and don't want you to change either.

It can cause emotional challenges for you to have the strength to follow your heart and soul for fear you may lose relationships with people you care about. If you lose them because you evolve and change, sadly that will be their choice.

It is important to surround yourself with caring and supportive friends who encourage you to be your best self. When you finally find your tribe, it can foster tremendous growth, both personally and professionally.

Some women seem to naturally attract others to them, but for others, its more challenging. Before you find your crew, you must know yourself. You don't know with whom you resonate with if you don't know what your core message is. Become comfortable with yourself and from there you will attract people that best match your ideals and are interested in your ideas.

Don't change yourself to fit in a model, be yourself and become your own model. You will feel valued and most successful with a tribe that best matches the qualities you imbibe.

Search out activities being offered in your community that interest you and join new groups of like-minded individuals. Networking groups provide opportunities to make connections and even friends and activities you enjoy that you didn't even know would be on your radar. Fight away any apprehension or fears and be open to new adventures.

Spend time indulging in your favorite activities and places. People who enjoy your favorite pastimes are candidates for great friendships.

You should never need to change to fit in. Natural friendship chemistry is just that, natural. Treasure your connection with individuals whose friendships develop easily and you feel comfortable with.

Continue to learn and evolve and share your passions with others. The world needs your contributions for the greater good of all.

Spend Time With Girl Friends

Just because you are grown up doesn't mean you don't need the enjoyment of spending time with your friends. Sure you have adult responsibilities, maybe continuing education, a job or two, a husband, children, a career, etc., but you still need to find time to be just "you", without all of the grown up roles you have to play.

When we were young we had friends we could be our real selves with, be silly with and tell our problems and dreams to. We still need friends like that. We need girlfriends we can commiserate with, tell secrets to, ask their female opinions, share girly books and movies with and go shopping with. Your girlfriends accept you, they don't judge you. Girls love to talk. We talk about our feelings. We can pour our hearts out to our girlfriends, we can purge built up emotions, frustrations and fears. We build each other up, encourage and support one another. Life is happier with girlfriends.

Spending intentional time with other women recharges your feminine energy in a big way. Make time for your own divine specialness and your divine sisters. When we are with other women we become more feminine, more attractive, alive and loving. Surround yourself with other women and be open to new friendships. Enjoy the power of femaleness.

Women's Circles

> *"Part of healing the wounded feminine and reclaiming feminine wisdom is for the women to reconnect, to come together as sisters with a common mission rather than stay isolated and reinforce a divisiveness which disempowers us all and weakens our efforts"* Jane Hardwicke Collings

Finding or building a community of like-minded women can really help to strengthen your relationship with feminine energy. Attending or creating women's circles can help to build this type of supportive and loving community. It can also be very healing to communicate and share the things that are happening in your life with other women. The feeling of sisterhood with other women is incredibly healing.

Now is the time for women to come together and support each other. The time of jealousy, competition, and rivalry amongst women needs to stop and will come to an end with your help.

There is evidence of spiritual ritual gatherings occurring possibly as early as 300,000 years ago in Middle Paleolithic societies, although little is known about the complexity of these gatherings. Actual evidence is found that communities gathering for spiritual and shamanic experience have been evidenced in the Upper Paleolithic societies, long before modern humanity. Although there is no written history, there is evidence of ritual art, paint, and other religious ceremonial relics, including the first representations of the revered female form. This means that human beings have been gathering in purposeful circle for a very long time, and that the central representation of divinity was feminine.

Women equally participated in circles around the fire for ritual and did the same as they prepared food for families and community. During these times they shared stories and tribal experience.

In many ancient cultures, women would retreat away from society during their "Moon cycle" which coincided with the occurrence of the New Moon. In some cultures, women would gather voluntarily in Moon lodges during their cycle to nest, embrace womanhood, and enhance their mental, physical and spiritual health. A time to share stories, rest, heal, nurture their bodies and the sacred bond of womanhood. Moon lodges or red tents as they are commonly referred to, were a safe space for girls to become women. As many may forget, like clockwork our usual cycle is almost perfectly in sync with the Moon. Upon their first period, girls were invited into the red tent society to learn from the generations that preceded them how to take care of their cyclic nature as a woman.

Ancient "moon cycle" rituals included chanting, adorning in red, face and body paint, womb massage, indulging in sweets, creating a sacred altar and telling stories of warrior women and goddesses. So what happened between then and now to make women's circles all but disappear from conventional culture? We weren't allowed to come together because it made people feel uncomfortable, and we were persecuted for it.

In 1484, the *Hammer of Witches* publication by two German Dominican monks began the systematic destruction of women's spiritual practices and health care by torturing and murdering women healers and spiritual leaders. This oppression lasted 500 years and was carried with colonialism to every corner of the Earth.

That didn't completely stop women from getting together on their own terms, from sewing and quilting circles to tea dates and Mary Kay parties. We were still called to gather, but we weren't allowed to dip into an energy that would offend the power of the masculine.

Women are awakening. We're remembering our roots. A remembrance that runs through our blood. This is why when we gather in circle it feels like coming home. Your blood remembers.

In circle we are all equal. No one is above another. You realize that you are not alone with what you're experiencing in life. Everyone is going through something. You see yourself in your sisters stories. In their pain, realness, triumphs and tears. You realize that no one has it all together and that life is messy and complicated. And that's OK.

Stepping into circle feels completely natural. That's because coming together in circle is completely natural. It's gaining more popularity nowadays but this isn't something new. Women have been gathering in circles for thousands of years.

There is a lot of shame, guilt, and stigma around sharing deep thoughts and emotions. This needs to be normalized in order to stimulate the feminine consciousness, which is what the world needs. Empathy, kindness, compassion, non-judgment, nurturing interactions, openness, creativity, and softness comes with strong Feminine Energy.

At first it can feel vulnerable to let your guard down and step into circle. The mistrust among women runs deep. For generations women have been pinned against each other. We have seen each other as our competition. We have been taught to gossip, judge, and put each other down.

In the Circle, we are all equal. There is no one in front of you and there's nobody behind you. No one is above you; no one is below you. The Circle is Sacred because it is designed to create unity.

Psychologists have proven that endorphins (the hormone of love and well-being) are released into our brains when we talk about ourselves. Some say that's one of the many benefits of therapy. In some women's circle, they start with a "Check-In", where each woman gets 10 minutes to be fully heard by the group. She can use this time to talk about anything on her mind.

The rest of the women give their full and raptured attention without interruption. To be heard by a group of women who you know loves you deeply, feels absolutely glorious. Women can share freely without fear of judgment, in an environment that feels completely safe and supported. Practicing the art of listening deeply also gives us a chance to tap into our empathy and patience, keeping us present in the moment without thinking about how we will respond.

Sharing your experiences with others can yield powerful revelations. Seeing friends deal with the same life challenges you have, makes you realize you are not the only person with these problems.

We all have times of low self-esteem, conflicts at work or in our relationships, of feeling challenged by parenting, money, or health.

When we meet in circle we join to hold everyone in sacred space and purpose. We are bringing forth an ancient way of connecting into modern times. We gather to share stories, to deepen our identities individually and in group, often with the intention to enable and shape a post-patriarchal way of being.

We also gather to heal. We can meet in circle to share our joy, we can meet in circle to work on projects or join in ritual at various levels of depth and purpose, and we can meet in circle to help to change our world.

When we see each other transform our life challenges into opportunities, we feel stronger than ever. We are reminded that we can do the same. When we are stuck in our own problems, it can be difficult to see the light at the end of the tunnel.

There are many kinds of circles depending on the needs of the members; they can be support circles, healing and wellness circles, spirituality circles, or action circles. In Native American women's circles, there was a talking stick and storytelling, a lot of sharing and listening. Per Jewish tradition, the circle is open lighting a candle and asking everyone to state her mother's and grandmothers' names. A Shamanic circle may involve drumming and journeying. Others may incorporate yoga, meditation, singing, moon rituals, fire ceremonies, astrology, etc.

Regardless of the style, the main purpose of a women's circle is to bond in sisterhood. Many women experience loneliness, depression and anxiety. Joining a women's circle that you relate to will change your life. You will find friends, acceptance and non-judgement. Find friends you can have deep conversations with, friends you can cry with, friends who support your life goals and believe in you.

This kind of connection and community is incredibly joyful and healing.

Romantic Relationships

*"She wouldn't let others define her; she
wrote her own story and she lived it."*

Your Life, Your Story, Your "Once Upon A Time"

Your "Once Upon A Time" is now.

You are the main character in the story of your life.

You are the storyteller of your story. You can change the story anytime.

You are the heroine of your story. Don't write yourself as the victim.

Don't allow anyone to make you the secondary character in your own book.

A Goddess Would Not Allow a Man to Consume Her or Control Her

- If he doesn't call, go to sleep.
- If he doesn't message, put your phone away and have a fantastic day anyway.
- If he tries to teach you a lesson with the silent treatment, ignore him completely.
- If he says unforgivable things and threatens to leave you after every argument, walk away from him.
- If he forbids you from doing things you love, walk away from him.
- If he plays with your feelings constantly, walk away from him.
- If he tries to insinuate that you don't need your friends now that you have him, spend more time with your friends.
- If he tries to tell you what to wear all of the time, walk away from him.

- If he wants access to your phone and emails, walk away from him.
- If he is jealous and doesn't trust you, walk away from him.

When a man is truly interested in you, there will be no need for you to do the pursuing. Men are born to pursue women. Yes, you can pursue a man if you want, but in most cases that is an obvious sign that he's not into you.

It's not natural for a man to sit back and let the woman do all the work. For a man who claims to like you to sit back and allow you to do all the calling, texting, date arrangements and talks about the future, it's pretty obvious where you stand in that man's life. When a man really wants you, you won't have to chase after him, you will be his priority.

Never beg a man to give you the things you know you deserve. The right man will give you everything you deserve and more. He is worth waiting for. Don't settle for less than you deserve or want.

You can't love a man into loving you. It doesn't matter how pretty you are, how loyal or loving you are, how well you treat him or how much attention you pay to him. You can't keep a man who doesn't want to be kept by you. Know when to walk away and stop wasting your precious time.

Live your life for yourself first. He is a secondary character in your story. Don't allow anyone else to be the main character in your Once Upon a Time story.

Disengage From Toxic Relationships

You're in a relationship to be happy, to smile, to laugh, and make good memories, not to be constantly upset, to feel hurt, and to cry.

It's hard to see what's best for yourself when you're invested in a relationship. It's not always easy to remember who you are and what you want. You can start to lose yourself and forget to make yourself and your happiness a priority.

Just because someone desires you doesn't mean they value you. Don't be impressed by a man's desire for you. Of course he wants you, you are beautiful and smart and kind and fun. You are divine! But it doesn't mean he is right for you just because he likes what he sees.

There's nothing wrong with admitting a relationship has run its course. Even if you can't imagine your life without that person, with time and distance, you'll be able to see the relationship for what it was: toxic as hell.

Signs You're In A Toxic Relationship And It's Ruining Your Life

- Passive aggression
- Jealousy and the blame game
- Criticism and contempt
- Arguing without communicating
- Negative energy
- Avoiding each other
- You're not yourself
- Feeling like there's no point
- You only think about making him happy
- You can't seem to do anything right
- Growth and change are seen as negatives
- He doesn't like you working or socializing
- Reminiscing about the beginnings instead of looking toward the future
- You're just not happy anymore

Women stay in toxic relationships hoping things will change and get better. They wont. They are waiting for a miracle that will never happen. Walk away! If someone is trying to control you, that is not love.

There are currently catch phrases to encourage you to let go of the past and create a new future, such as;

- Release what is no longer serving you
- Change your belief system and change your life
- Love yourself, take care of yourself, put yourself first
- Be the heroine of your life. Not the victim.

> *"Women are not rehabilitation centers for badly raised men. It is not your job to fix him, change him, parent him, or raise him. You want a partner, not a project." Julia Roberts*

The divine is extremely sensitive to negative energy. As women, we deeply value our relationships.

We want to be nurturing to our romantic partner, our friends, our children, and our loved ones. Quite often, this can lead to co-dependency or unhealthy relationships where we give too much of ourselves and expect little in return.

Just because someone is "family" doesn't mean you have to tolerate lies, chaos, dramas, manipulation and disrespect. Detachment doesn't mean not caring.

You must understand that some people never really grow. They never learn their lessons. They never recognize their mistakes, they never acknowledge their faults, they never admit when they are wrong.

You will never receive an apology from them, and you will never see their behavior change.

Characteristics of Toxic People:

- Talk badly about others
- Are negative
- Lack compassion

- Take up way to much of your time
- Constantly have drama going on
- Lie to you
- Criticize you
- Talk more than listen
- Play the victim
- Lose their temper
- Have to be right
- Treat others poorly
- Are self-obsessed
- Try to control you
- Have addiction issues

Rise Up

Rise up and unleash your Inner Goddess. Let no man put you down, humiliate you, hold you back or make you think you are weak or unworthy. Believe me, men are more afraid of you than you know.

Their day of control and domination of the Divine Feminine is coming to an end. As they lose control they roar louder. When you rise up you make it easier for your sisters to follow your lead so they too can rise up and be all they can be.

You were not created to live depressed, defeated, guilty, ashamed, condemned, or unworthy. You were created to be victorious.

If you are in a toxic or abusive relationship with anyone, make the decision today to take a step back.

You can love them from a distance. Walk away from the practice of pleasing people who choose to never see your worth.

Seek out positive, uplifting, encouraging relationships with people who recognize your value. A healthy relationship doesn't drag you down. It inspires you to be better.

The Differences Between your "Soul Mate" and "Your Twin Flame" and Your "Life Partner"

These are 3 archetypal love relationships which humans experience. Understanding these love connection types can help you have peace with the fact that different relationships are meant for different reasons.

Life Partner

All love relationships before have prepared you to recognize and call in your life partner. A life partner is someone you have true love for. You know you've found your life partner when you've identified a real, unconditional love for another and they have expressed and shown it towards you. It's all about love. Both partners, as individuals, have done the work to become a whole person, so you are two whole people coexisting. There is a lifestyle match, you want to live the same life.

Soul Mate

A soul mate couple are two individual souls that have connected with each other through many lifetimes, in order to teach each other lessons and fulfill karmic debts. Soul mates usually feel like they have met before and play deep roles in each other's lives. A soul mate does not have to be romantic, rather you can have a sibling, friend, or parent be a soul mate in your life.

Soul mate relationships can last a lifetime, or just a few months. Depending on the contract between the two, your soul mate could only be in your life for you to uncover a karmic lesson. For instance, the first love of your life could be a soul mate. Even though you were highschool sweethearts, and eventually went separate ways, that person was in your life to teach you lessons you never learned before. The same goes for a best girlfriend, turned stranger. You both were connected so strongly for a period of time to teach each other valuable soul lessons. If you no longer talk, or have a relationship, it's possible that your soul contract with that friend ended.

Twin Flame

Though twin flame pairs tend to be romantic, they could also be platonic. But a twin flame isn't about love, it's about truth. Twin flames can often cause radical personal awakenings for one another because they can see straight through to one another.

According to Dr. Lisa Vallejos: *"The real purpose of Twin Flame is not about great sex, emotional highs and an epic love story, it's to wake you up, shake you up and call you higher. It is a gift presented by the Divine, one you can only grasp fully when you've released all the smaller things you've been clinging to for so long, that no longer serve you."*

They're a perfect match, most specifically with regards to the internal challenges they face, so meeting one another head-on is like being able to face yourself and work through your internal issues.

In this way, while a life partner is about cultivating a deep connection through love, a twin flame is about cultivating a deep connection through shared pain, understanding, and the growth that comes from that. It's really about cutting away the layers of noise to get to the truth of your life and all things as a whole.

Even two people who are made for one another, life partners through-and-through, often cause each other quite a bit of pain along the journey of their relationship. It's inevitable when two people seek to come together in such an intimate fashion that conflict would arise.

However, a twin flame is, to some degree, supposed to cause us pain. Without any pain inflicted, we're probably not going through any real transformation.

It's in the very definition of intense personal growth that one must experience great pain to realize a great transformation. The pain experienced in a typical relationship with a life partner can and often does help us grow, but it's more about learning to work together between one another and live with one another.

A life partner and twin flame can both be very long term relationships. However, a life partner is by choice whereas a twin flame is not.

We decide to spend our life with a life partner. But a twin flame is the kind of person that leaves our life, comes back, leaves again, and always ends up coming back to us (or us back to them). That is, until each person has "burned" away their baggage, whatever specific baggage the connection revolves around.

That's the one caveat to the "eternal" connection one develops with their twin flame: it may take quite a long time, but it will end if the root cause for the connection is healed. At least, the need for a recurring physical connection will end.

Our twin flame helps us grow, and we them, by unearthing our deepest feelings of pain and inadequacy. Physical proximity works as a catalyst for this growth, dissolving all those false or misconceived internal structures until only the truth remains, the truth about ourselves and our place in the world.

Until this happens, twin flame-type relationships can often appear bound to one another, their shared pain and general life experience bringing them together until the healing is complete. A twin flame does not make a good life partner.

I have had several clients come to me wanting me to help them cut the cord binding them to their twin flame, usually because they are confused and frustrated with a yo-yo romantic relationship, "cutting the cord" is temporary. It will end only if the root cause for the connection is healed.

There is a lot of contradictory information written about twin flame relationships, which too often gets confused with soul mate relationships.

Signs You May Have Met Your Twin Flame

- You feel like you've met this person before; this might manifest itself as a deja vu. They feel very familiar and you feel deeply connected them.
- They make you feel as though you're "home" and their presence makes you feel safe.
- You instantly establish an intense connection and can't get enough of each other.
- You feel at ease to be yourself, your authentic self, without fear of judgement or rejection.
- You challenge each other and they bring about significant transformation in your life.
- They make you a better person and vice versa.
- You may come in and out of each other's lives but you're somehow always pulled back to them.
- Your relationship can be rocky sometimes but you're always there for one another.
- Your love for each other isn't necessarily romantic, but it is unconditional.
- They expose you to different perspectives and you think differently when you are with them; you feel a sense of awakening.

Marriage

"A woman who creates a full, happy life on her own is much more inviting than one who looks to a man to create it for her." Mandy Hall

In some ancient cultures marriages were arranged, in others the woman had more say in who they married. Of course there was love, attraction, and infatuation, but the dynamics of a marriage were different than we know it in our modern western culture.

Families lived in clans so the extended family of siblings, parents, grandparents, aunties and uncles and cousins were in close proximity to the family unit of husband, wife and their children.

The business of living and staying alive required hard work, the workload was lighter with more helping hands, a helping hand and a listening ear was never far away. Women stuck together and tended to the daily business of women and socialized with other women while the men were away for the day taking care of their responsibilities and socializing with other men.

An ancient Divine Feminine woman did not expect her husband to necessarily be her best friend, intimate confidant, soul mate, emotional support, intellectual equal or comfort in times of sorrow. Instead women got emotional support and opinions from other women. Kinship and friendship was at arms reach for them whenever they needed it.

I believe human beings are meant to live like this, in loving communities, close friendships and relationships, around nature every day, growing our own food and creating art. Not working day and night to the point of exhaustion and live isolated from our extended families, like we do in modern society.

We have high, sometimes impossible, standards when looking for future husbands. We have high expectations in our marriage relationships wanting our husbands to be our everything, all the time, forever. Where expectations are high, disappointment is sure to follow. I'm not suggesting we lower our standards but we do need to be more realistic about the business of marriage.

When we are young with not much experience, and probably not many good role models, we tend to be idealistic about our views on marriage and relationships. It is to our detriment we have not been taught as young women about our divine selves and our ancient history.

The divine feminine and divine masculine have different energies and powers. When you come to understand, love and honor these differences you will not expect the impossible from your mate or make demands in your relationship which he isn't comfortable accommodating for very long.

We need to find or create a tribe of like minded divine feminine women to befriend, socialize and collaborate with. We need to have lives, interests and friendships outside of a marriage. We need to be happy, whole and fulfilled divine feminine women on our own and not expect our husbands to fulfill all of our needs. He will love you more and respect you more when you are confident and independent rather than feeling you are needy, clingy and emotionally dependent on him.

When you are confident and comfortable with who you are and stand firm in your divine feminine you will have an understanding of the differences between the divine feminine and masculine energies.

One of those being, him as the giver and you the receiver. When a man is in his divine masculine role he falls in love when he can give to you, not because of how much you can give or do for him.

Feminine energy is about "being' instead of "doing". When you focus on simply being in the moment and enjoying a man's company and attention, you automatically shift your vibe so that he can step into the masculine, "doer" role. To do that you must be open to receive. So resist the temptation to prove your worth by giving, and instead create the space for him to give to you.

When you become a mother, you understand the more you care for and do for the child, the more you love them. Give your husband the opportunity for the same experience. Give him the opportunity to learn to love and care more deeply for you and his children.

If you want him to love you more and bond to you more, allow him to give to you and do for you. He will love you and feel good about himself. Men enjoy being with women who make them feel good about themselves. One of the main reasons for infidelity and men leaving their wives for another woman is how the "other" woman makes him feel about himself versus how the complaining, unappreciative wife makes them feel.

Relationship with Divinity

For a very long time, we've been led to believe that God is male. The language we have to describe this God: that "He" created us and that He is "our Father". All the depictions we've been shown of this God, in paintings, murals and sculptures made over millennia, are of a male, sitting up in heaven, surveying "His" creations.

I'm not here to tell you that it's not true. I'm here to offer another, additional piece of the picture.

God and the Goddess

There are at least two principles involved in creation. Everyone who knows basic biology knows that two counterparts are required for life to form: man and woman, male and female and in the divine realms, God and Goddess. Both are necessary and both are vital for the different physical and energetic qualities they bring. But for the last 13,000 years, the divine feminine and divine masculine principles that are so fundamental to the healthy creativity and ongoing survival of our planet have been wildly out of balance. That's not to say there has been too much of one principle and not enough of the other. The divine masculine has also been a victim of our history and its long patriarchal rampage.

Just as expressions of the Divine Feminine have been systematically silenced and destroyed for almost as long as we have kept records, so have the most sacred aspects of the masculine. And in their place, the patriarchal "God" and His systems of society have instead taken root. So it's important, I think, to make it clear that the return of the Goddess doesn't mean the appointment of a counterpart to the "God" we know and recognize. The Goddess comes to pave the way for the Divine Masculine to also return.

What Happened to the Divine Feminine?

When the patriarchy arrived the Goddesses were turned from living and present allies to myths and stories which were only allowed to exist in the mind. The sacred rituals and practices the ancients used to draw their power down were suppressed and stopped or hidden by necessity. Gradually, over time, humans became removed from their Goddesses and their counterpart Gods, and instead, they were presented with this alternate, singular "God" to put their trust in.

It's important to not underestimate the detrimental impact on the lives of the ancients caused by the direct suppression of their sacred beliefs and ritual practices. It was understood then, that connection to and communion with the Divine Feminine needed to be an embodied experience. The dances, rituals, ceremonies, symbols, tools, elixirs, medicines, plants and repeated actions directly involving the Earth and nature, were what allowed Her power to move through her people. It was the physicality of their actions which kept the Divine Feminine alive.

One way to truly reclaim the sacred feminine principles in your life, is to get out of your head, and back into your body. Move your feet. Dance. Stand up straight and inhabit your muscles, joints, organs, your bones and your blood. Your body has a wisdom of its own, which is directly connected to the sacred feminine. Live from your heart, trust your intuition and unleash your personal Inner Goddess.

Your Inner Goddess is not a destination, there is no "aha" to aim for. Her gentle re-emergence is a process and She will reveal to you everything you want to know, in the language that She speaks.

CHAPTER 8

The Seasons of Your Divine Feminine Life

"I have resolved to live, not just endure each season of my life."

Our divine life on earth is precious, every bit of it, every stage of it. Appreciate where you are in your journey, even if it isn't where you want to be. Every season serves a purpose. Life is passing rapidly, we are only here for a short while.

Enjoy and embrace the season you are in because it will change. Be ready to accept the season that you are about to enter. Your spirituality will change with your spiritual seasons just as the earth changes with the natural seasons. Embrace each season because each one has special purposes.

Life is a continuous progress. We all grow, develop and mature. As we continue to move on in life, we move from one stage in life to the next. For some, this transition feels like a natural process, while others find themselves stuck in certain stages for decades. Some might even skip entire stages completely, without learning the important lessons of a given stage. Fear of change is something that plagues many of us. Giving ourselves permission to grow and evolve may take some practice.

Western society is fixated on the beauty of youth, society starts overlooking older people, especially women, whose value is often judged based on conventional beauty standards, which makes it difficult for some women to easily pass from one stage of life to the next, for fear of losing their youth and relevance.

Coupled with the physical changes women experience when aging, this can throw you into feelings of confusion, helplessness, and frustration made even more difficult when old ways of dealing with things no longer seem to work. Motivations that used to carry you through tough times give way to deeply buried longings from an earlier time.

Investing in yourself, in your personal growth, in your well-being and your happiness, is not self-indulgent, it's not selfish, it's a must. Revising your life plan, changing lanes or just changing is fine. For instance, the person you are at 28, 38, or 48 is not always the same person you were at 19 when you chose your major in college or the degree you were going for.

The real purpose of your different stages of life is that your soul, the deepest most essential you, is calling you to create a more authentic expression of yourself: who you were born to be. In each stage you are letting go of parts of your old life. The initial phase of any transformation is the process of dissolving all that is no longer needed, that which will not be part of the new life ahead.

Inner transformation begins by dissolving the roles you have been playing, that no longer serve you, so you can be "reborn" into a more meaningful and fulfilling expression of your true self. We are many people in one lifetime.

The Mischievous Maiden

The Maiden is the young girl, before child-bearing years, usually depicted as a teen. However, technically the Maiden is also a girl in her infancy and childhood, as well as adolescence. She is your youth, your new beginnings, your birth. She is Spring, when the earth has just awakened from a long slumber.

The Maiden is seen as the virginal young woman, or girl, who has not yet awakened. She is all about enchantment, youthful ideas and enthusiasm. These are your fun flirtatious teenage years when your body magically changes from a girl to a woman, the budding seductress.

The Beauty of Being a Mother

> *"The female being has been chosen by the Creator*
> *to be the portal between the spiritual realm and the*
> *physical realm. The only force on earth powerful*
> *enough to navigate unborn spirits onto this planet.*
> *So, tell me, why do we not treat her as such?"*

With our modern liberation, new found freedom and opportunities it suddenly somehow became not okay, and even embarrassing, to be just a mother and wife. If you choose to focus on a family instead of your career, it may seem you've given up on feminism and your rights as an enlightened woman.

You may even feel a bit guilty like you are contributing to the evil patriarchy that is designed to keep you in the kitchen and changing diapers. Nothing could be further from the truth.

The beauty of our new age is that we have the freedom to make choices for ourselves. We can choose what makes us happy and what kind of life we want to live. Even with the injustices that still exist there has never been a better time to be a women.

The unique blessing that only women have, is the ability to create life and bring beautiful babies into the world. You will never know a greater love than when you hold your new born baby, that just came out of your womb, that is literally a part of you, your flesh and blood. It is a miracle, a joy and a blessing to be a mother, when it is of your own choosing.

Loving, nurturing and teaching children is a full time job, a career in itself. It is an honor to be a mother, an experience like no other. The world needs mothers to bring forth kind, enlightened children to change and save our world. We need mothers who love being mothers.

The Great Goddess was a mother, revered for her ability to create life and nurture children, there is no greater calling. The womb of a woman is the most sacred place on earth. When you believe this, when you know this, you cannot allow an unqualified man inside.

Gone are the days when women don't have the opportunity to get an education or the choice to pursue a career or choose to never marry. Today we have choices. If your choice is to be a full time wife and mother and enjoy your life on your terms, don't let anyone make you feel bad about that. If others wish to be in the corporate world or own a business, it is also wonderful that they have the opportunity to do so. But it is not their right to think choosing motherhood is a lesser position in life. If women have a support system they can do whatever they wish, have children and a career and rule the world! Be joyful you have choices and honor other women's choices, even when they are different than yours.

We all get to be who we are. We each have our own femininity, divine purpose and specialness about us to contribute love, change, and balance into our lives, our families and the world around us.

The Crone "The Crowned One"

*"The crone has earned that title. She offers sage
advice and tested wisdom. She is secure in her
skin, her soul and self. She shares her knowledge
freely. She is beautiful. She is trustworthy. She
is my friend. I adore her and rely on her."*

See your future self; a beautiful face graced with history, a
healthy vibrant body and a clear sharp mind. Trust that this is
the best time of life.

The Celtic tradition honors three passages in a woman's life;
Maiden, Mother, Crone. As Crones we have integrated the tender
aspects of the maiden, the many lessons of mothering and the
rich experience of a life long lived. Still, all are a part of the whole.

It was formerly a terrifying view to me that I should one day
be an old woman. I now find that Nature has provided pleasure
for every season of life. As uncomfortable as it might be, change is
both inevitable, and important. Our souls are in physical bodies
living many lives from infancy to old age, if we are fortunate
enough to live that long.

The first half of our lives are usually spent living the life the
world has imposed on us and by society's standards and rules. We
are consumed with schooling, careers, family, mortgages and bills.
Our time is owned by our employers, children and spouses. As we
contemplate the second half of our lives we have the opportunity
to make new plans and new goals to design a life of completion
that gives us satisfaction and fills our soul with peace.

Let's not hang on to shallow worldly concepts of who we
should be or how we should look. May we be wise enough to
enjoy each season of our life, especially our older years as spiritual,
powerful, influential teachers and leaders just as our ancient Divine
Feminine Shaman and Wise Old Oracles were. Don't mourn or

cry over your lost youth, move on to the next season of your life with excited anticipation of a new life to explore.

What ever life you have lived it has been yours. All the moments of your life have made you who you are now. It is your unique history and no one else's, it is part of what makes you special and unlike anyone else. As you reflect on the first half of your life do so with love and gratitude for all of the people who have entered into your life story and those you have loved.

Naturally there have been hard times, loss and regrets. But it doesn't help to sit around regretting our mistakes, we can't go back in time to change anything. But we can use our experiences as life lessons to go forward and create the second half of our lives with wisdom and purpose.

As we approach the age of retirement we can do so on cruse control without much thought, as an extension of our past life, either riding on the coat tails of our success or living with regrets and dreading old age. Either way we are stagnant without further progress. Or we can develop a rich new life with the perspective of creating a completion to our life which will give us joy and satisfaction.

Our bodies will age, our skin will loosen, our tummies will bulge, our breasts will sag, that is the cycle of life, but our soul never ages or grows old. Our Inner Goddess encourages us and allows us to spend our time meaningfully until the last moment of our life. When we live from our heart and soul we are the masters of our destiny.

Begin by asking yourself what is the life your soul wants. What is in your heart, not your head? What kind of life will bring your soul joy? Ask yourself again and again. Close your eyes and go within, at some moment the answer will come. Once you've found it, resolve to do your best to realize the dream you really want, making the most of the precious time you have left on Mother Earth.

CHAPTER 9

Goddess Self-Actualization

A tenacious grip on our own ideals, irrespective of hurdles, would propel us towards self-actualization!

Fully unleashing your Inner Goddess and self-actualization is a lifelong process, it comes bit by bit as we experience and conquer life's challenges and opportunities. Growth never ends until the journey of life is over.

A self-actualizer is a woman with a desire to reach her full potential and a strong sense of fulfillment.

She focuses on bigger things than just herself. She tends to see the big picture instead of considering only herself, and may dedicate her life to a mission, or cause, or deeper purpose.

Actualization is in the final stages of development when a woman is able to take full advantage of her talents while being mindful of her limitations. It is also referred to as enlightened maturity characterized by the achievement of goals, acceptance of oneself, and the ability to self-assess in a realistic and positive way.

Self-actualization is about how open a woman is to growth and health rather than ideals such as perfection or success. Once esteem needs, such as self-confidence and self-respect have been met, a woman might begin to self-actualize.

Women are in the best place now, more than ever to evaluate this level of being. Today women have the luxury of being more self-sufficient, which means we have the agency to choose for ourselves what needs we want to pursue and in what order.

Self-actualization is our power that we posses which can help us accomplish almost anything we want.

The needs associated with self-actualization include:

- acceptance of facts
- lack of prejudice
- ability to solve problems
- sense of morality
- creativity
- spontaneity

Self-actualized women:

- accept themselves and others
- have a well developed sense of creativity, sometimes referred to as a "creative spirit"
- maintain deep and meaningful relationships
- can exist independently, have an appreciation for solitude
- have a sense of humor, particularly an ability to find humor in their own mistakes
- accurately perceive reality, have an easier time detecting falseness in others
- have a sense of purpose and perform regular tasks geared toward that purpose
- experience frequent moments of profound happiness
- demonstrate empathy and compassion for others

- have an ongoing appreciation of the goodness in life, the trait of childlike wonder
- are comfortable with the unknown, keep an open mind

Examples of Self-Actualization

Self-actualization may manifest in many forms, and some of how a self-actualized woman may appear can depend on her age, culture, and other factors. Behaviors might include:

- finding humor in a given situation
- getting enjoyment and satisfaction out of the present moment
- understanding what they need in order to gain a sense of fulfillment
- tendency to feel secure and unashamed in who they are

Self-actualized women don't sacrifice their potentialities in the service of others; rather, they use their full powers in the service of others. Everyone has to find their own unique ways to hear the inner wisdom that can help them live their life of truth in a way that utilizes their strengths, while taking steps to achieve their dreams, both large and small.

Self-actualization is not a one-size-fits-all goal. No two women are exactly alike, so everyone will have a slightly different path. Take each day as it comes and keep an open mind.

As human beings we have the desire for personal growth and development throughout our lives. By accomplishing self-actualization, you are able to find meaning and purpose in life and you will be able to say you truly "lived".

As you develop spiritually and unleash your Inner Goddess, so does your self-actualization. You will become the Goddess you are in training for.

CONCLUSION

"She remembered who she was and the
game changed." Lalah Deliah

As you work on finding and connecting with your Inner Goddess you will simultaneously have opportunities present themselves which will allow you to add your contributions to the betterment of our world.

To help reshape the world, we need to lead like women, not be bad clones of men, and our divine feminine traits are the pathway to bring corrective balance to the world.

The Divine Feminine woman is:

- Confident and doesn't need validation from others.
- She embraces her age, color, shape and size and honors her divinity.
- She is able to balance her ability to listen and nurture with her ability to drive and control.
- She is able to lead with authority, and at the same time show her vulnerability.
- She cares for people as much as she cares about profits.

Grab onto that passion of yours, be it;

- Rescuing animals
- Fighting for no kill shelters
- Feeding and helping the homeless
- Jailing men who abuse women and children
- Stopping human trafficking
- Environmental pollution
- Saving the rainforests
- Teaching sustainable living practices
- Helping 3rd world countries
- Promoting fair healthcare, natural healthcare, preventive healthcare
- Teaching holistic and natural health
- Providing a loving, safe, child or pet daycare center for mothers while they work
- Placing a warm meal in front of a homeless veteran
- Showing a struggling child how to read a story or solve a math problem
- Visiting the local shelter to play with the animals waiting for a loving home
- Planting more trees
- Stopping factory farming
- Supporting local small farmers
- Supporting the organic food movement
- Marching for the rights of others to vote, work, worship and exist in peace and safety
- Use your legal training to bring justice
- Use your business savvy to structure fairness in business practices
- Use your medical training to over throw greed and return to healing
- Use your political influence to rid our society of power hungry individuals, companies and industries, etc,

Whatever your passion is, it will be your piece of the puzzle to help bring corrective balance and Divine Feminine Energy to the world.

Unleash your Inner Goddess, this is no time to be small or timid, we have moved past that. It doesn't serve you or the world. Now, more than ever we need to use all of the knowledge and tools available to us to step out of our old roles and into our true Divine Feminine potential.

Each of us, like cells in the human body, carry a special piece of the energy that makes up the greater whole. The outside world can affect us, and we can affect it.

There is nothing that can't be fixed, changed or saved when we have the powers from the unseen world guiding and assisting us. However you reach the heavens and they reach back to you, through prayer, meditation, journeying, dreams or intuition, just do it, it makes no difference, it is all the same. One of my favorite old Chinese proverbs is "There are many paths to the top of the mountain, but when you get there, the view is always the same". Meaning there is no "one" way or "right" way for everyone to accomplish the same outcome.

There are many ways to accomplish the same end. So be sure to cheer your sisters on in their work, even if it looks different than yours. Divine Feminine Energy is about tolerance, love and acceptance of those who are different than you are. A good heart is a good heart, don't judge. They will have influence and reach people you can't.

Let your Inner Goddess guide you. Find your passion, your contribution and reason for being on earth at this time. Never forget your divinity. Fight for justice. Fight for love. Fight for yourself. Fight for humanity. Heal yourself and Mother Earth. Become the Warrior Goddess. And so it is. To be continued in volume III, Extreme Feminine Self-Care....

ABOUT THE AUTHOR

Marilyn Pabon is a dedicated researcher in all areas of natural health and wellness and ancient ancestral wisdom. She is passionate about supporting women in ways that will be most relevant and useful for them in today's world by modernizing ancient wisdom.

Marilyn is the author of the Divine Feminine Handbooks I, II, II, and IV. Before she started writing books she worked as a Natural Wellness Consultant and Educator, Detoxification Facilitator, Energy Worker and Emotion Code Practitioner removing trapped emotions. Her mission now is to help women harness their own creative power, self-esteem and personal potential so they may become the Divine Feminine they are meant to be.

She is a California native currently living in Utah's beautiful red rock country at the gateway to Zion National Park with her husband and daughter.

For more information about her work and books, visit: www. marilynpabon.com

SHARE THE DREAM

Divine Feminine Handbooks I, II, III, and IV are more than a set of books.

It is a lifestyle and movement in which modern women can live to their greatest and truest versions of themselves. It's a dedication to empower women to break free from the shackles of outdated and limiting beliefs. It is a call to awaken the Divine Feminine Energy in us all. It is a remembrance of our divine ancient foremothers who once were revered as creators of life, healers, spiritual guides, shamans and leaders.

If you too have a dream of helping your divine sisters learn of their sacred heritage and cultivate their goddess within, so they too can live empowered fulfilling lives, please share these books.

One of the simplest ways you can do that is by leaving a review online. Write down your thoughts about the book on your favorite book selling or review sites so that other Divine Feminine women can be inspired to know more.

You can also share your ideas on your social media page. Make sure to include the official hashtag:

#divinefemininehandbooks.

From my heart to yours,
Marilyn Pabon

Printed in the United States
by Baker & Taylor Publisher Services